# BOW VALLEY SPORT CLIMBS

John Martin & Jon Jones

Rocky Mountain Books

*Front cover: Barb Clemes on Success Pool (12a), Grotto Canyon photo courtesy of Brian Bailey*



The publisher gratefully acknowledges the assistance provided by the Alberta Foundation for the Arts and by the federal Department of Communications.

Published by Rocky Mountain Books
#4 Spruce Centre SW, Calgary, AB T3C 3B3
Printed and bound in Canada by
Kromar Printing Ltd, Winnipeg

**ISBN 0-921102-22-4**

**Canadian Cataloguing in Publication Data**

Martin, John, 1947-
Bow Valley sport climbs

Includes index.
ISBN 0-921102-22-4

1. Rock climbing–Alberta–Bow Valley–Guidebooks.
2. Bow Valley (Alta.)–Guidebooks. I. Jones, Jon II. Title.
GV199.44.C22A45 1993 796.5'223'0971233 C93-091395-7

# TABLE OF CONTENTS

*Dave Dornian on The Warlock (12a) Carrot Creek, photo Jon Jones*

# INTRODUCTION

This guidebook provides complete topo format coverage for all the main sport climbing areas in the Bow Valley from the mountain front west to Banff. In addition to information drawn from the earlier guidebooks *Bow Valley Update* and *Bow Valley Rock*, it includes some 175 new routes completed at Carrot Creek, The Stoneworks, Cougar Canyon and Grotto Canyon since the publication of *Bow Valley Update*. It also covers new areas that have only just begun to be developed.

Information on the many multi-pitch, "traditional" style climbs in the Bow Valley can be found in *Bow Valley Rock*.

## THE ROUTES

The majority of routes covered by this guide are sport climbs with all-bolt protection and chained anchors; however, some of the older climbs require gear and/or lack good top anchors. Some of the older routes were not cleaned to today's standards and may have loose rock. Virtually all the routes established since 1988 (see index) have been carefully cleaned; however, it should be kept in mind that the nature of the rock, repeated freeze-thaw cycles, and the passage of climbers may subsequently cause some holds to loosen.

All the climbs in this guide are on limestone, mainly of the Eldon, Livingstone and Palliser formations. Don't be put off by the appearance of some of the rock — most of it climbs better than it looks. The cliffs vary from steep slabs to overhanging walls, with the majority being vertical or nearly so. Cracks and pockets are rare at most of the venues, and the climbing is mainly on small edges, layback flakes and underclings. Crux sequences are often technical and hard to "read", making on-sight ascents seem hard for their grades. Overall, there is a distinctive "feel" to the climbs quite unlike anything to be found away from the Rockies.

## GRADES OF DIFFICULTY

The routes are graded using the standard Yosemite Decimal System, minus the "5." prefix. Route grades range from 5.6 to 5.13b, with some 80% of the climbs being in the 5.10 and 5.11 range. All grades are for on-sight ascents. Grotto Canyon has more climbs than any of the other areas, with all levels of difficulty being well represented. Cougar Canyon is particularly good for the 5.9, 5.10 and low 5.11 grades, while Carrot Creek has the best selection in the 5.11 to low 5.12 range.

## TOP ROPING

The climbs described in this guidebook have been designed specifically for leading, not for toproping. It is unsafe to attempt to set up a toprope on some of these climbs, both for yourelf and for others. In fact it can be ***DEADLY*** - as witness the recent toproping fatality (yes fatality) in Cougar Canyon. Three other good reasons not to toprope — erosion, vegetation damage, and rock polishing — are discussed below in the section on environmental awareness. The vast majority of the climbs in the guide can be climbed safely from the ground up. In a few cases, safety can be facilitated by stick clipping the first or even the second bolt. If you feel you must toprope, please do it at a climbing wall or at an established toproping venue such as Wasootch Slabs. Illusion Rock (in Grotto Canyon), which has already been beaten to death by topropers, is perhaps an exception to this general suggestion.

## GEAR

A 50m rope and about 8 quickdraws will get you up and down most of the routes in this guide. Some of the longer climbs require up to 13 quickdraws (or even up to 19, for some of the route combinations) and 2 ropes (check topos for rap/lower lengths). The numbers of bolts indicated on the topos should be accurate, but take enough quickdraws to allow for one extra just in case. A small rack of RP's, Rocks, TCU's and Friends (or equivalents) will suffice for the routes that are not completely equipped. Specific gear requirements are noted where necessary in the main body of the guide.

## FIXED PROTECTION

Bolts on the older climbs are 5/16" self-drill concrete anchors with shear and pull-out strengths of about 2000 kg. More recently, the somewhat stronger 3/8" Hilti Kwik-Bolt has taken over as the standard installation on new climbs. The home-made aluminum hangers found on some routes have been tested and will hold about 1900 kg; home-made steel hangers are likely somewhat stronger. Chain installations range from 1/4" to 3/8". The authors are not aware of any bolt, hanger or chain failures at any of the climbing areas covered in this guidebook.

## QUALITY RATINGS

The quality ratings are based on a system of 0 to 5 stars. Wherever possible, the ratings are based on a consensus of climbers who have done a large number of the guidebook routes. The 5 star rating is reserved for a very few (ten) climbs considered to be the best in the area. Zero star climbs are not necessarily turkeys and may be no worse than undistinguished. A few climbs are, however, described as "not recommended", either because of loose rock or because they cannot be adequately protected. No quality ratings are given for climbs that have been manufactured or that have deliberately enhanced holds, or new routes about which little is known.

## FIRST ASCENT INFORMATION

First ascent information is given in the index. When a single name is given, it is that of the person who constructed and first led the route (in the case of rap-bolted climbs), or who led the first ascent (in the case of a ground-up route). Two or more names are given in cases where more than one person contributed significantly to the final product.

## WEATHER

The climbing season in the Bow Valley generally lasts from April to some time in October, although episodes of non-climbable weather or unsuitable rock conditions (i.e. lingering dampness or snow) can be expected during this period. In good years it may occasionally be warm enough to climb as early as March or even February, or as late as November. The canyons tend to be colder than the rest of the Bow Valley because of shading, wind funnelling and cold air drainage (a shallow layer of relatively cold, dense air that typically flows down the canyon bottoms in the morning and late afternoon). Staying in the sun, out of the wind, and out of the canyon bottoms are the keys to comfortable early and late season climbing.

## TICKS

Rocky Mountain wood ticks are locally abundant in the guidebook area from April (occasionally as early as February) until mid June. They seem to favour warm, dry, south and west-facing exposures. Wood ticks are small (5 mm), flat, 8-legged, reddish brown, slow-moving creatures that like to crawl up humans (and animals) looking for a meal. They are easily removed before they attach themselves, which usually doesn't happen for several hours. After a tick is attached to the skin it can still be removed, although with more difficulty. However, since some sources indicate that tick "bites" can have unpleasant health consequences (note, though, that wood ticks are not known to carry Lyme disease), it is better not to let any get attached. A good tickbusting routine is to inspect your gear, your clothing and yourself (especially the nape of your neck and other hairy areas) before leaving the climbing area. Insect repellents containing a high concentration of DEET (check the label) are said to keep ticks off. If you find a tick that has managed to hitch-hike into your home, flush it down the toilet.

## THEFT

Thefts from climbers' cars have been uncommon to date in the Bow Valley, although a few car break-ins are known to have occurred. There have also been some thefts of gear from routes.

## LOCAL SERVICES

Canmore, the focal point of climbing in the guidebook area, is a large town with all the conveniences of modern life (except a climbing shop — for that you have to go to Banff or Calgary). Overnighting possibilities at Canmore include the Alpine Club of Canada Clubhouse (turn north off Highway 1A on Indian Flats Road, about 1 km east of the Trans Canada Highway interchange). Gas, food and lodging are also available a few kilometres east of Canmore on the Trans Canada Highway, at Dead Man's Flat. On Highway 1A, gas and food can be found at the Heart Mountain Cafe in Exshaw. Public campgrounds are operated by the Province of Alberta at Bow Valley Provincial Park (near Yamnuska) and at three locations along the Trans Canada Highway: Lac des Arcs, Three Sisters and Bow River. In case of emergency, contact the Canmore detachment of the RCMP at 678-5516.

# ENVIRONMENTAL AWARENESS

Climbers and climbing have an impact on their physical and social environments. These impacts are becoming more and more noticeable as the number of climbers skyrockets, and our activities are coming under increasing scrutiny by land managers with the power to restrict or possibly even ban our sport in some areas. The climbing media are full of access horror stories, either actual or potential, from other areas. We are not immune here; if we are not successful in regulating our own activities, others will be more than happy to do the job for us. Thus, it behooves each of us to promote the image of sport climbers as responsible and environmentally aware individuals and of sport climbing as an activity that can co-exist with other land uses on a self-regulated basis. The guidelines below may be helpful in this regard.

1. **Safety.** Never forget that you are responsible for the safety of anyone your actions may affect — for example, a passing hiker who may be unaware of your presence. ***EXTREME CAUTION*** is required in this regard at the tops of cliffs, many of which are sloping, rubbly and very dangerous. For your own safety, consider wearing a helmet when climbing.

2. **Litter.** Sometimes it isn't enough to just pack out your own litter. Take out anyone else's you find as well. Keep in mind that webbing, slings and ropes left on climbs may be perceived as litter, especially in areas popular with hikers.

3. **Human Waste.** Human waste is becoming a serious problem in the cramped confines of the more popular canyons. If you must shit, walk outside the canyon and go at least 50 feet from the nearest watercourse. In Cougar Canyon it may not be practical to leave the canyon, but the 50 foot rule still applies. Ideally, you should be prepared to pack **everything** out. Otherwise, at least burn your toilet paper.

4. **Pets.** Give everybody a break — don't bring your dog unless you arrange to have it supervised at all times. Unsupervised pets can contribute to water contamination and are often a nuisance to others.

5. **Water contamination.** Drinking from any of the streams in the guidebook area is not recommended as the water may be contaminated. Follow the guidelines given in points 3 and 4 above in order to avoid adding to the problem.

6. **Erosion and Vegetation Damage.** The soil and vegetation communities in mountain environments, ours included, tend to be fragile and easily damaged or destroyed. This is particularly true on steep slopes, such as those leading to the tops of cliffs — a good reason not to toprope. Damage also occurs in valley bottoms, so please stick to established trails.

7. **Rock Polishing.** Although to the uninitiated the rock resources of the Bow Valley may appear to be virtually inexhaustible, the number of areas suitable for sport climbing development is in fact quite limited. The main limiting factor is rock quality. All the climbs in the area are on limestone, a soft rock that polishes easily with repeated foot traffic. Several of the more popular cliffs (especially Illusion Rock, in Grotto Canyon) have already become very polished and slippery, making for unpleasant climbing. In most cases this has largely been caused by excessive toproping, often by beginners whose sloppy footwork is particularly damaging. By flailing on routes, or encouraging others to do so, you hasten the degradation, if not the destruction, of our limited rock climbing resource — so please give the rock and your novice partner a break by not insisting that they dangle and paddle their way up something out of their league. So far as anyone knows, the polishing process is ***IRREVERSIBLE.***

8. **Camping and Fires** If you camp in non-designated areas, please follow low impact camping procedures. Good books on the topic are available. Please don't camp in Grotto or Cougar canyons, neither of which has sites suitable for the purpose. Note that camping is illegal in the portion of Cougar Creek valley downstream of the canyon, which is privately owned.

9. **Courtesy and Crag Etiquette.** Carrot, Cougar and Grotto Canyons are now very crowded with both climbers and non-climbers, especially on weekends. Consider others. They probably don't want to have to walk around someone or their gear when it is blocking the trail, or to be forced to listen to climbers swearing and being rowdy. When non-climbers ask you a question, think of it as an opportunity to make a good impression for both yourself and our sport. Be considerate of other climbers too — follow common-sense guidelines, such as not hogging routes and not leaving ropes on routes you aren't climbing.

10. **Alteration of Existing Climbs.** Upgrading of fixed pins to bolts, installation or upgrading of belay anchors, and removal of loose rock are encouraged on existing climbs. However, please contact the first ascensionist for consent before making any other alterations, such as the addition, subtraction or relocation of protection points.

11. **Theft and Vandalism.** Removing gear from climbs is theft, and in some cases it may endanger others. Enough said.

12. **Vigilantism.** Vigilante activities to protest the climbing activities of others are ultimately futile or worse. Reasoned discussion usually works better.

# GUIDELINES FOR NEW ROUTE CREATION

The following guidelines for new route creation represent a majority consensus among the local climbers most active in new route development. As indicated, they are guidelines, not rules (except in the case of national park regulations).

1. Remember that your route will stand as a very personal statement of your attitudes towards others.

2. Avoid squeezing in a route if it will compromise the integrity of an existing climb.

3. Safety should be a priority. Clean all loose rock from the route thoroughly. Be aware of potential hazards and avoid endangering others during the cleaning process. ***ALWAYS WEAR A HELMET.***

4. The chiselling, drilling, or creation by other means (including glue) of new holds is illegal in the national parks and not acceptable in other areas. Enlargement or enhancement of existing holds is not acceptable either. It is recognized that there is a gray area between cleaning and enhancement; navigation through this uncharted area is by individual conscience.

5. Reinforcement of existing holds with epoxy is illegal in the national parks. Opinion is divided as to its acceptability elsewhere.

6. Avoid unnecessary clearing of vegetation. Tree cutting is illegal in the national parks. In areas outside the parks, tree cutting should be avoided, particularly in areas popular with hikers. A mature tree (say 6" [15 cm] or more in diameter — let your conscience be your guide) should certainly never be sacrificed for a climbing route.

7. Work the moves carefully before installing the bolts so that you get the placements right the first time. Don't forget about climbers who are not as tall as you are! Provide enough protection to minimize the risk of injury. ***THE ROUTE SHOULD BE SAFE FOR AN ON-SIGHT LEAD BY A CLIMBER COMPETENT AT ITS GRADE.*** Consider the initial two clips with particular care; the best option may be to install a relatively high first bolt that is intended to be stick-clipped.

8. Use appropriate equipment. Bolts should be comparable with those on recent existing climbs; i.e. 3/8" (or 10mm) x 3" (76 mm) or longer. Do not use pitons, as these often loosen with time and can easily fail. It is considered OK to place a bolt beside a crack, except perhaps in the rare cases where all or most of a climb can be safely protected with non-fixed gear. It's also OK not to put a bolt beside a crack. Install a permanent anchor at the top of the route, rather than some tatty piece of webbing or rope. Glue-in ring bolts or permanent rap hangers are preferred. For chained anchors, 5/16" chain is recommended. If you bolt the chains

directly to the rock, rather than attaching them to hangers, use bolts that are 3-3/4" (95 mm) or longer to compensate for the thickness of the chain and washers. Avoid using a tree as the top anchor if possible; if there is no other option, chain the tree (remember when cutting the chain that you need a fair bit more than the circumference of the tree — both to avoid a three-way pull on the chain closure and to allow for tree growth).

**9.** In popular areas, camouflage fixed gear to reduce its obtrusiveness. Gray automotive primer works tolerably well and has much lower reflectivity than enamel paints. Paint the gear at home rather than after it is on the route, unless you plan to use a template.

**10.** Report the route accurately. Give it an honest grade for an **on-sight ascent** and list requirements for gear or stick-clipping.

**11.** Respect the efforts of other climbers. Stay off routes that are actively being worked (see point 12).

**12.** Don't leave your rope on a route between work sessions — the time saved is not worth the risk. Other good reasons: 1) it might be stolen; and 2) others may feel the rope is an eyesore. If you want other climbers to stay off the route while you work it, this can be indicated by simple expedients such as leaving off the bottom bolt hanger or attaching a red tag or an "under construction" note to the bottom hanger. Other climbers will respect your efforts as long as you are actively working on a route, but don't expect to monopolize a piece of rock indefinitely — after all, it is public property.

**13.** Painting route names on the rock is illegal in the national parks and strongly discouraged elsewhere.

## NEW ROUTE INFORMATION

Preparing a guidebook like this one is a big job. You can help by providing comments, corrections and new route information to the authors care of Rocky Mountain Books, #4 Spruce Centre SW, Calgary, AB T3C 3B3.

## ACKNOWLEDGEMENTS

The authors would like to thank the following people for their contributions to this guidebook: Gillean & Tony Daffern, David Dornian, Andy Genereux, France Gosselin, Lynda Howard, Bruce Keller, JD LeBlanc, Chris Miller, Simon Parboosingh, Geoff Powter, Bill Rennie, Jackie St. George - Rennie, Darren Tremaine, Mark Whalen, and Blob Wyvill.

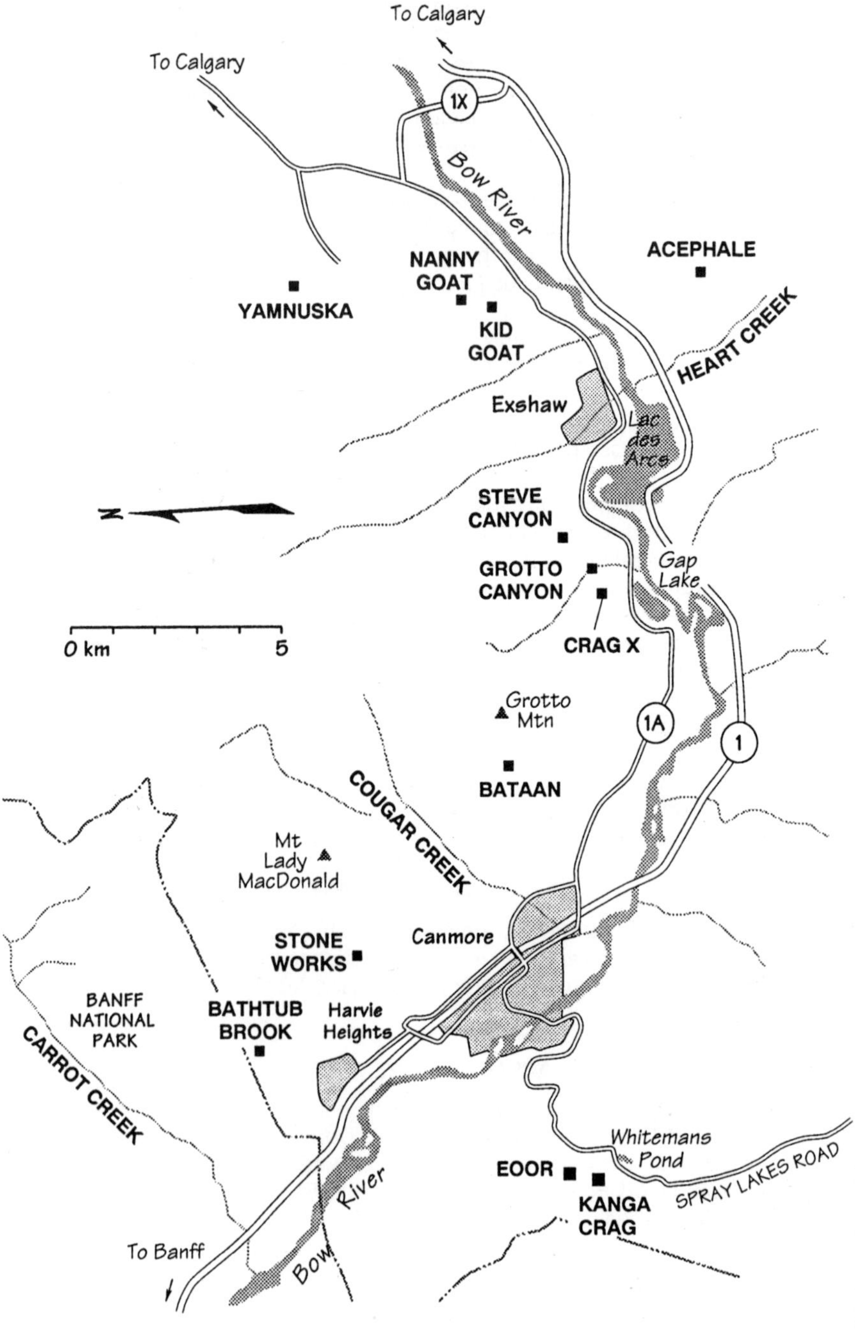
To Calgary
To Calgary
1X
Bow River
ACEPHALE
NANNY GOAT
YAMNUSKA
KID GOAT
HEART CREEK
Exshaw
Lac des Arcs
STEVE CANYON
GROTTO CANYON
Gap Lake
CRAG X
0 km
5
Grotto Mtn
1A
1
BATAAN
COUGAR CREEK
Mt Lady MacDonald
STONE WORKS
Canmore
BANFF NATIONAL PARK
BATHTUB BROOK
Harvie Heights
CARROT CREEK
Whitemans Pond
EOOR
KANGA CRAG
SPRAY LAKES ROAD
River
Bow
To Banff

# ACEPHALE

This new area is located on on the north side of Heart Mountain, about 45 minutes south of the Trans Canada Highway. At the time of writing, the only climbs completed were those on the left end of Lower Wall. There are several projects and lots of potential for new routes on very steep, pocketed rock to the right, where the cliff extends several hundred metres uphill. Acephale is in the shade for most of the day and the rock seeps after rainfalls, so it is best to wait for warm, dry weather before going there. Drinking water can be picked up at a large boulder, where the stream emerges from under the ground, about 5 minutes before the crag is reached.

## Approach

Park in the ditch of the eastbound lanes of the Trans Canada Highway, 1.2 km east of Heart Creek (100m east of the eastern end of the guard rail). A faint trail, which starts by a cairn at a dip in the embankment above, leads to a bridge on the hiking trail from Heart Creek to Quaite Valley. Cross this and continue up the stream bed to a power line. Take the trail underneath this a short distance east (left) to a prominent trail which comes in from the right. Follow this trail, taking the right hand fork wherever it branches, to a waterfall. Switchbacks on the left lead to a small slab which is crossed using a fixed cable. The trail now follows the drainage above the waterfall, crossing it several times, and leads to a large, dead tree across the dry stream bed near the start of *I'm a Lazy Man* on Lower Wall.

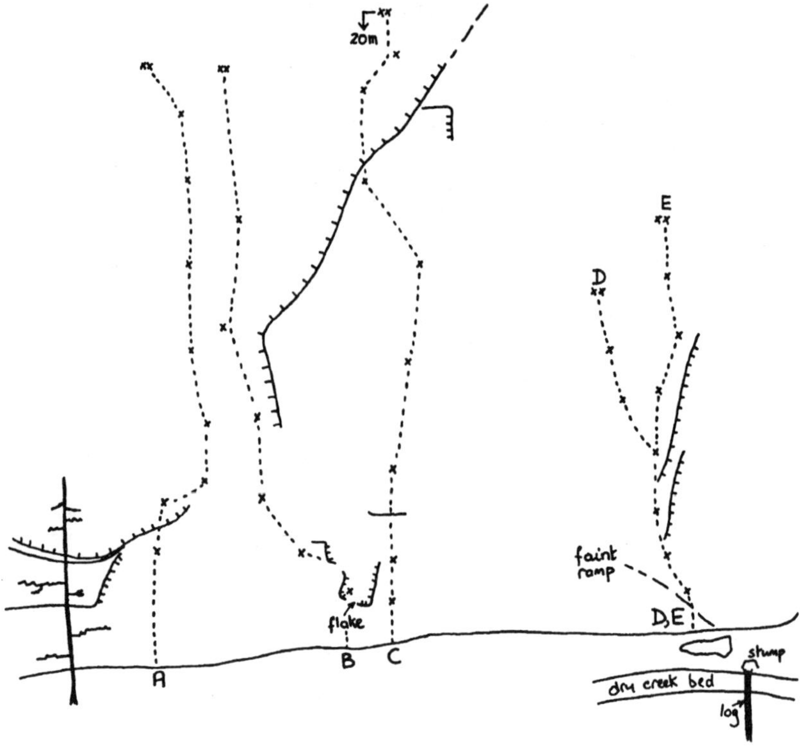


## LOWER WALL

| | | |
|---|---|---|
| A | Girl Drink Drunk | 12a |
| B | The Irradiator | 11d |
| C | Illy Down | 12a |
| D | I'm a Lazy Man | 12a/b |
| E | Surfer Poser | 11d |

# HEART CREEK

Heart Creek, which drains a narrow valley between Heart Mountain and Mount McGillivray, crosses the Trans Canada Highway just east of the Lac des Arcs interchange. It is perhaps the prettiest of the Bow Corridor canyon climbing venues, but because of the narrowness of the valley and the orientation of the cliffs, it is one of the chillier areas in spring and fall. The climbs were established in the mid-80's and some may seem a bit runout by today's standards. Take two ropes and a small selection of wired nuts and Friends. Routes listed as "not recommended" may require pitons.

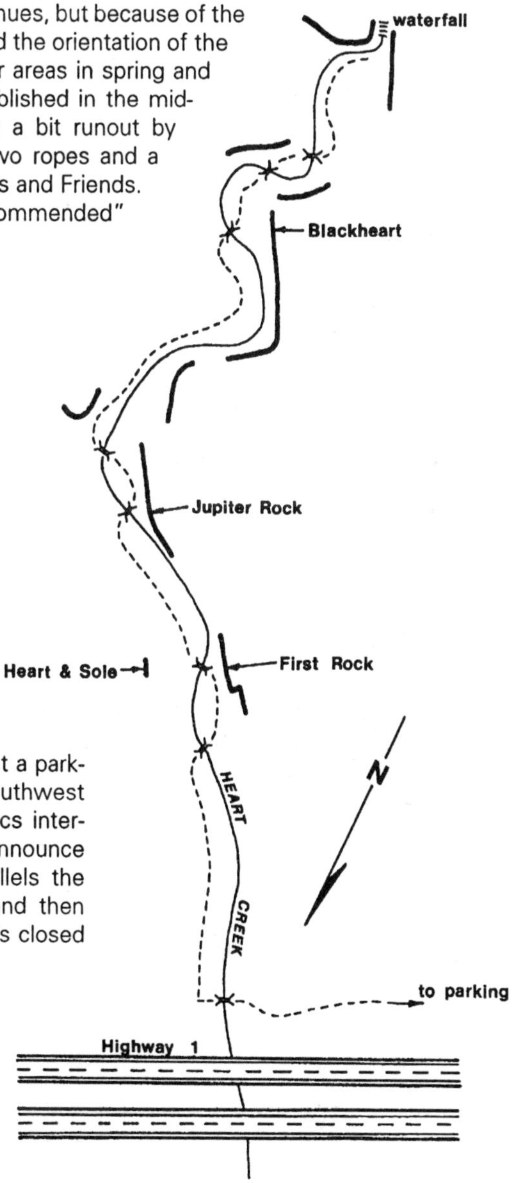


## Approach

A graded hiking trail starts at a parking area located in the southwest quadrant of the Lac des Arcs interchange. Highway signs announce the turnoff. The trail parallels the highway for about 700m and then continues up the creek. It is closed to bicycles.

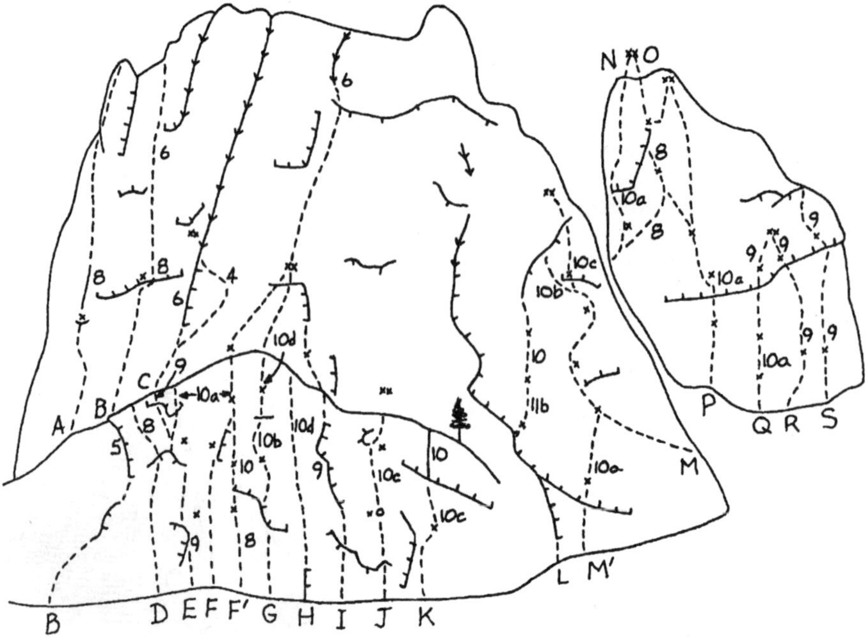


## FIRST ROCK

| | | | |
|---|---|---|---|
| A | Potentilla Pillar | 8 | not recommended |
| B | Heartline | 8 | small Rocks |
| C | Choc-a-Bloc * | 4 or 6 | gear to Friend 3 |
| D | Less Than Zero | 8 | small Friends |
| E | Back to Zero | 9 | |
| F | Feel on Baby *** | 10a | |
| F' | Feel on Baby Direct *** | 10a | |
| G | Dynamic Dumpling *** | 10d | gear |
| H | Caveling | 10d | toprope |
| I | Cavebird | 9 | not recommended |
| J | Midnight Rambler * | 10c | Friends |
| K | Honky Tonk Woman * | 10c | Friends |
| L | Bitch ** | 11b | gear |
| M | Sticky Fingers **** | 10c | |
| M' | Sticky Fingers Direct | 10a | |
| N | Dirty Work * | 10a | gear |
| O | Dandelions * | 8 | gear |
| P | Dead Flowers * | 10a | gear |
| Q | Brown Sugar * | 10a | Rock 4 |
| R | Heartburn | 9 | Friend 1 |
| S | Wild Horses | 9 | |

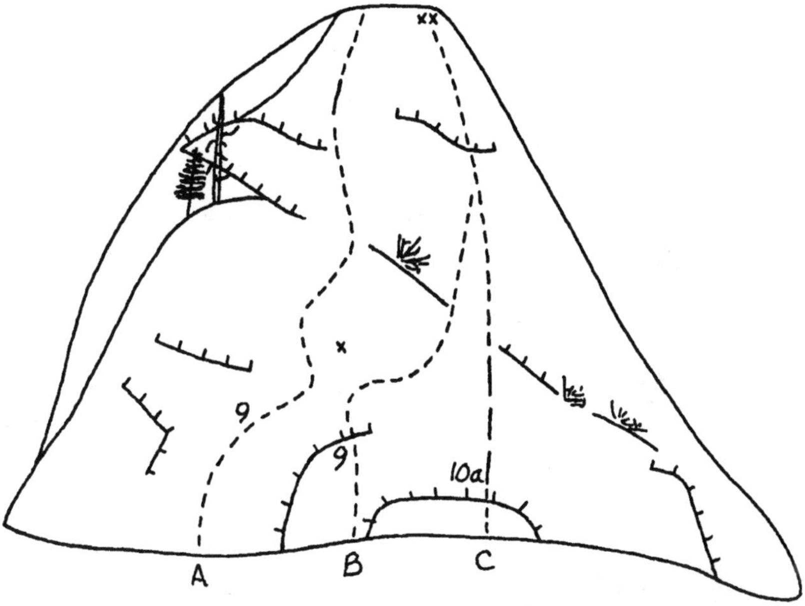


**HEART & SOLE**

| | | | |
|---|---|---|---|
| A | Sole Food | 9 | Rock 2, Friend 2 |
| B | Heart & Sole | 9 | RP 3 |
| C | Mr. Percival* | 10a | Rocks, RP 3, Friend 2 |

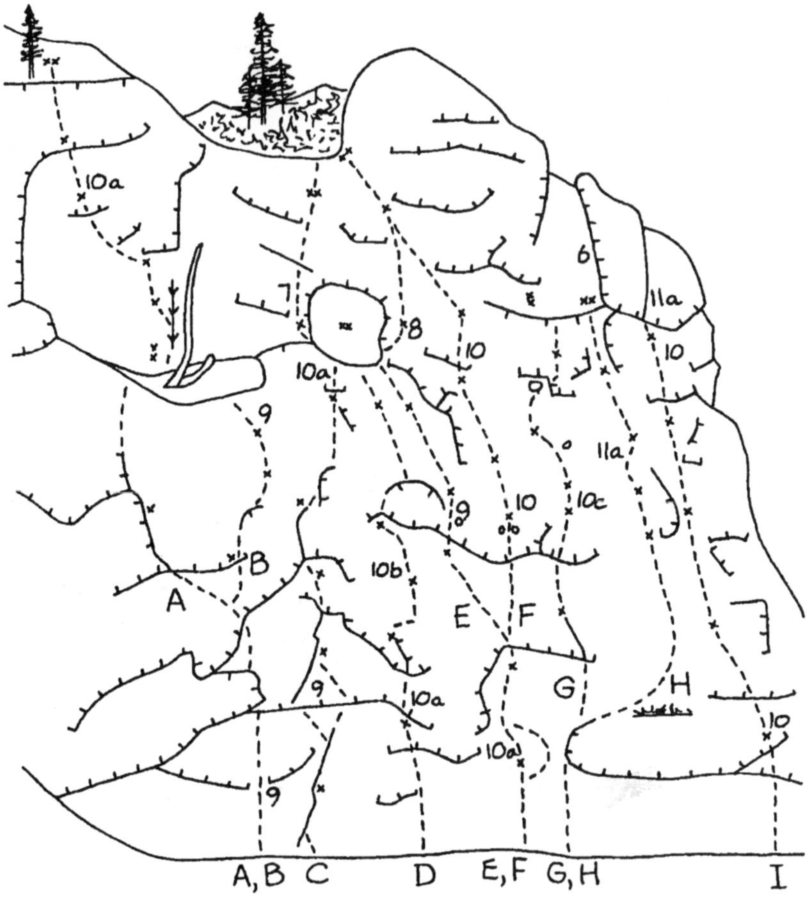


**JUPITER ROCK**

| | | | |
|---|---|---|---|
| A | Dark Chocolate | 9 | gear |
| B | Riparian ** | 10a | gear |
| C | Venus **** | 10a | gear |
| D | Brontes ** | 10b | gear |
| E | Callisto *** | 9 | |
| F | For Your Eyes Only * | 10b | gear |
| G | Puppet on a Chain * | 10c | gear |
| H | Heart of Darkness *** | 11a | gear |
| I | Heart of Gold | 11a | gear |

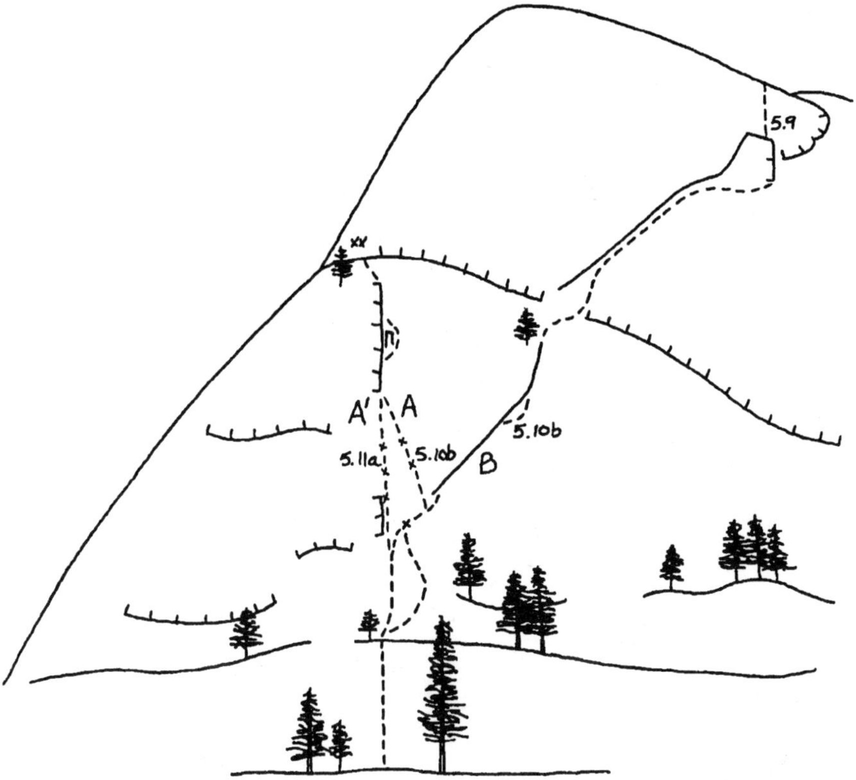


## BLACKHEART AREA

| | | | |
|---|---|---|---|
| A | Blackheart ** | 10b | wired nuts, Friend 3 |
| B | Blackheart Direct ** | 11a | wired nuts, Friend 3 |
| C | Heart Crack | 10b | not recommended |

## KANGA CRAG AND THE EAST END OF MT RUNDLE (EEOR)

The area's only multi-pitch sport climbs, True Grit and Parallel Dreams, are located at the left end of EEOR. Both routes are entirely bolt protected. The climbs on Kanga Crag are also fully equipped except for *California Dreaming;* not enough is known about them to assign them quality ratings.

### Approach

Take the Spray Lakes road south from Canmore to a pull off at the top of the big hill by a green shed (gauging station) beside Whitemans Pond (approximately 9km from Canmore). A trail 100m north (right) of here follows a sparsely treed, shallow depression up the hill to Kanga Crag, reaching it at *Rocky and Me* (10-12 minutes). To get to EEOR from here, follow the trail right, skirting beneath the right-hand end of Kanga Crag. After 5 minutes, the trail emerges from the trees and cuts directly across a talus slope. From here, the prominent triangular roof marked on the topo of EEOR is clearly visible. A short, steep section of trail leads up beside a large scree chute, which is crossed near its apex to reach the base of the climbs (20-25 minutes from parking).

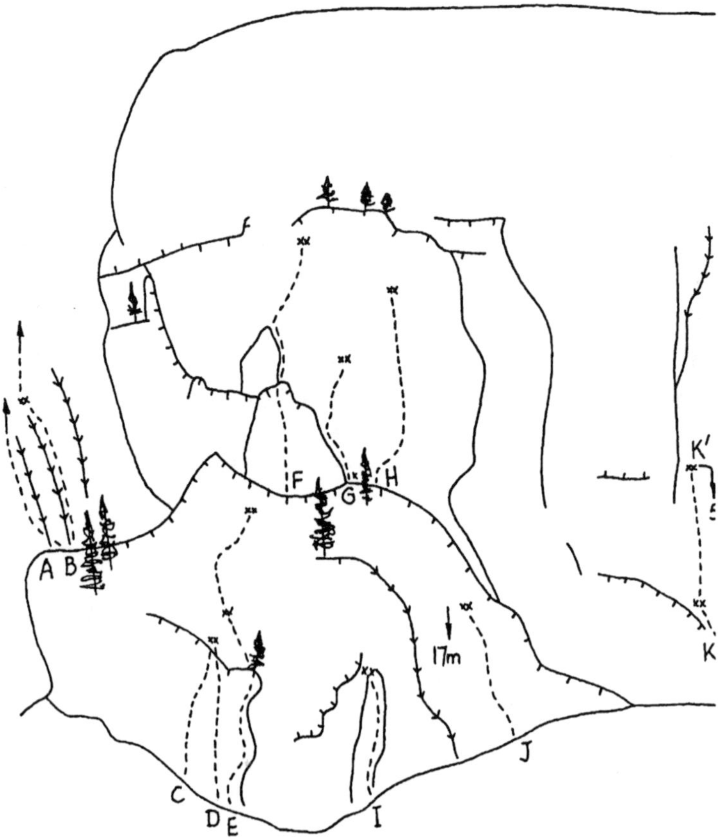

***CLIMBERS ARE STRONGLY ADVISED TO WEAR HELMETS WHEN CLIMBING ON EITHER KANGA CRAG OR EEOR BECAUSE OF ROCKFALL HAZARD.***

## KANGA CRAG

| | | | |
|---|---|---|---|
| A-I | projects | | |
| J | Riff Raff | 10a | 8 bolts |
| K | Canadian Air, pitch 1 | 11a | 9 bolts |
| K' | Canadian Air, pitch 2 | 12a/b | 10 bolts |
| L | Leave Your Hat On, pitch 1 | 11a/b | 9 bolts |
| L' | Leave Your Hat On, pitch 2 | 12a | 10 bolts |
| M | California Dreaming | 10b | gear to 3" |
| N | project | | |
| O | Rocky & Me | 10d | 9 bolts |
| P | Rub Me Right | 10c | 9 bolts |
| Q | Toucha Toucha Me | 7 | 7 bolts |

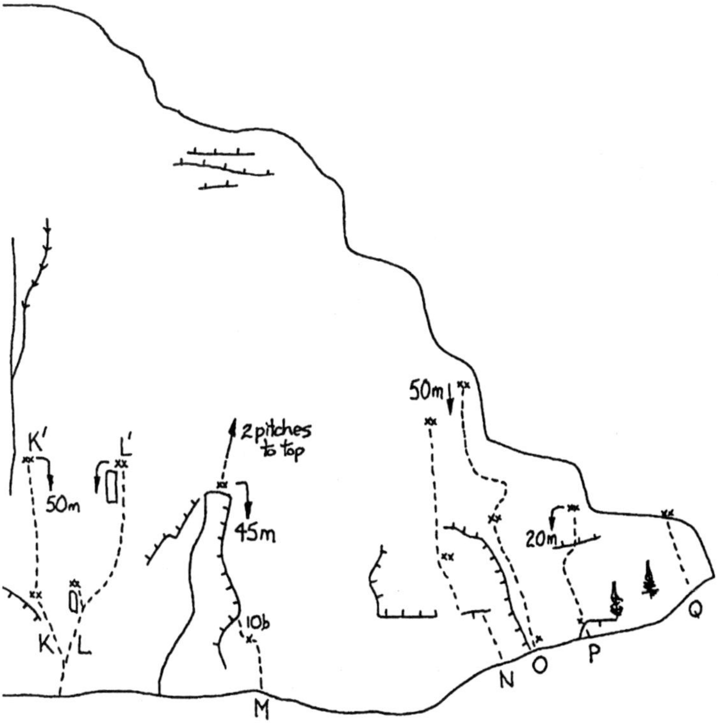

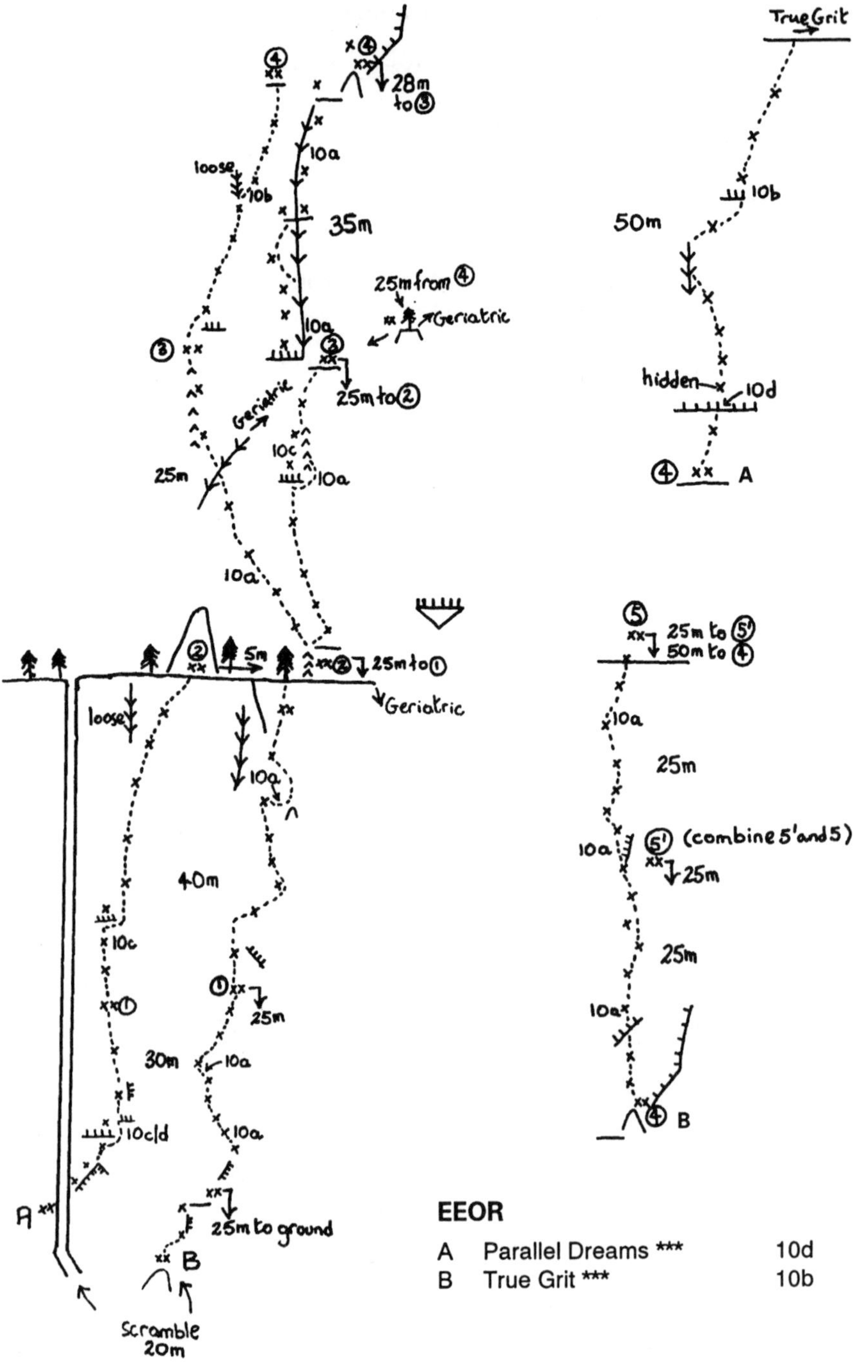


## EEOR

| | | |
|---|---|---|
| A | Parallel Dreams *** | 10d |
| B | True Grit *** | 10b |

# CAVE AND BASIN CRAG

This steep, northwest facing crag of Palliser limestone is situated on the northwest end of the Sulphur Mountain ridge behind the Cave and Basin Pool. The routes here are new and with the exception of The Raven have not had many ascents, and so quality ratings have not been given.

### Approach

Follow the wooden walkway behind the Cave and Basin Pool to its highest point. From here, follow discontinuous game trails and survey cut lines straight up the hillside for 20 minutes to slabs at the base of the crag. The routes start from a broad terrace reached by skirting right of the slabs.

### CAVE AND BASIN CRAG

| | | | |
|---|---|---|---|
| A | The Raven *** | 10d | 2 pitches (35m, 25m); 10 clips |
| B | project | | |
| C | The Masque | 11c/d | |
| D | Telltale Heart | 12b/c | |
| D' | project | | |
| E | project | | |

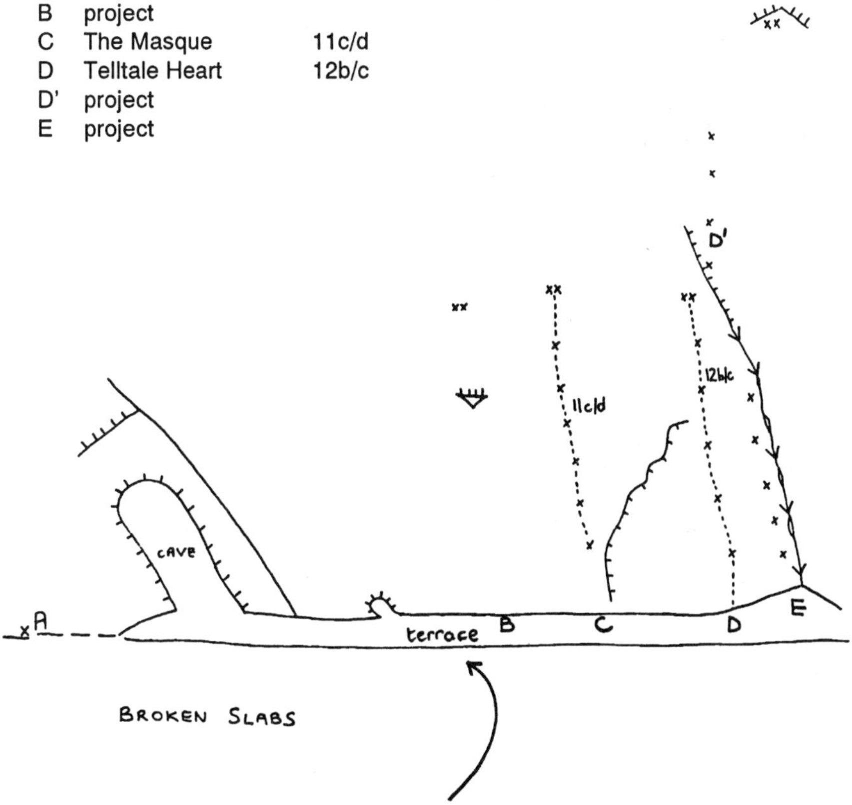

# CARROT CREEK

Carrot Creek boasts one of the highest concentrations of difficult climbs on local limestone. While there are now a few more routes here in the 5.10 grade, the bulk of the climbs are still in the 5.11 to low 5.12 range. The climbs are located in a gorge cut into Livingstone limestone, approximately 4 km north-east of the Trans Canada Highway. Because the gorge is so deep and narrow, temperatures here tend to be cooler than at other venues covered in this guide. The sun rarely reaches the rock on Raven's Nest Buttress, The Gully Wall and Graffiti Wall and the frigid waters of Carrot Creek keep the air there cool, even on the hottest of days. However, Sun City and Up the Creek catch the sun from late morning until mid afternoon and Muscle Beach, Westside Buttress, and The Embankment come into the sun in early afternoon. The recent development of these areas has extended the climbing season at Carrot Creek into early spring and late fall. The Entrance Wall and Small Wall get late afternoon and evening sun in summer.

The climbs are often smooth at the start, consistently steep and often overhanging, and usually sustained and strenuous. The descent from most climbs is by rappel. All can be descended in 25m raps, but ***extreme caution*** is advised if attempting this from the top of Raven's Nest Buttress as the steep angle makes it difficult to swing in to some of the intermediate rap stations. From the top of Raven's Nest Buttress, it is possible to descend by heading down the back side to a saddle and then south (right) to the start of the canyon.

Virtually all the climbs here are totally bolt protected. Of those that are not, only *Problems With Guinness* is highly recommended, and this requires only a 3.5 Friend.

### Approach

Turn right from the west-bound lane of the Trans Canada Highway at a signpost marked "Carrot Creek" (1.6 km west of the Banff Park entrance). From the parking area it is a pleasant 40 minute walk through open woodland to the gorge. Bikes are useful (but illegal) on the first three quarters of the trail. Makeshift bridges have been built where needed, but these sometimes wash out during spring floods and it may be necessary to ford the creek. On leaving the car park you ***must*** turn right (west). There is a break in the centre median 1.3 km farther west.

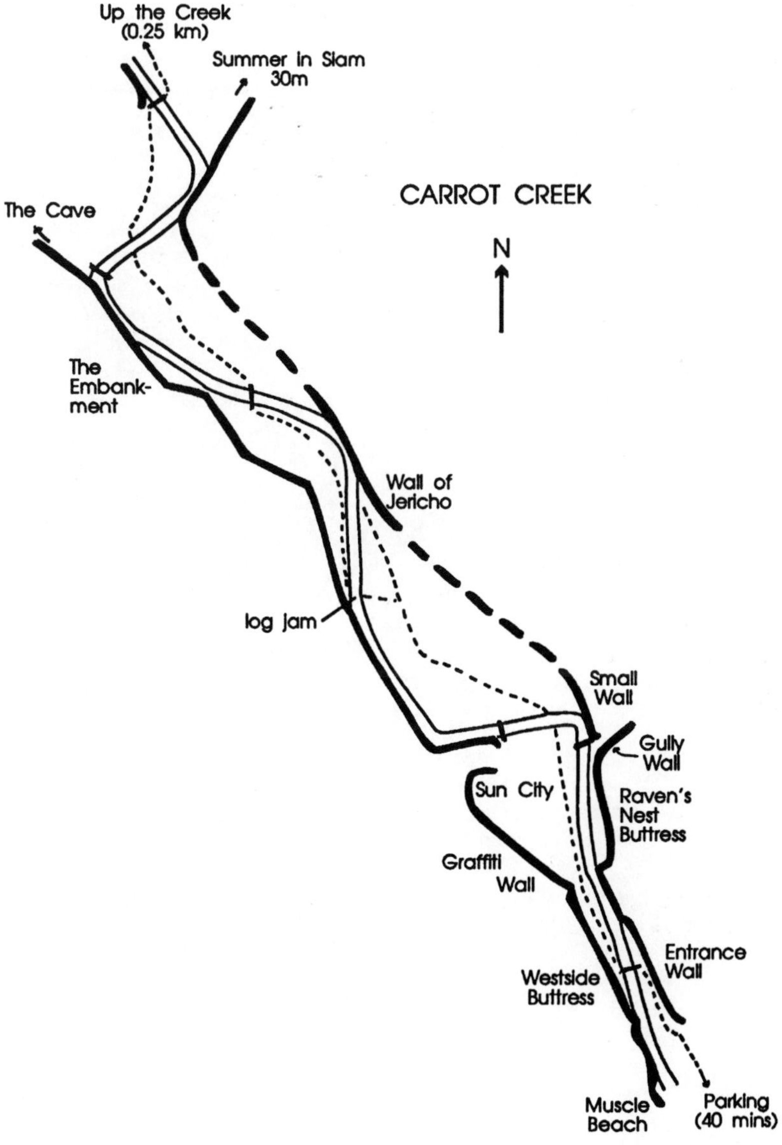
CARROT CREEK
N
Up the Creek
(0.25 km)
Summer in Slam
30m
The Cave
The Embankment
Wall of Jericho
log jam
Small Wall
Gully Wall
Sun City
Raven's Nest Buttress
Graffiti Wall
Entrance Wall
Westside Buttress
Muscle Beach
Parking
(40 mins)

*Bill Rennie on Muscle Beach (11d), photo Jon Jones*

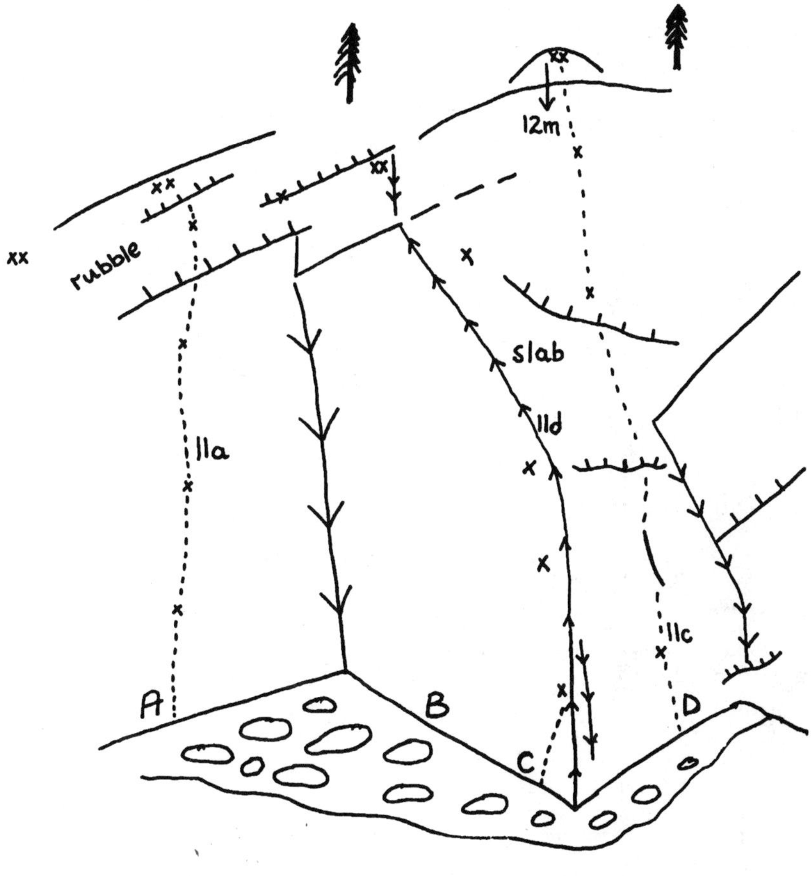


**MUSCLE BEACH**

| | | | |
|---|---|---|---|
| A | Hard Bodies * | 11a | |
| B | project | | |
| C | Muscle Beach ***** | 11d | |
| D | Beach Balls | 11c | 0.5,3.5 Friend |

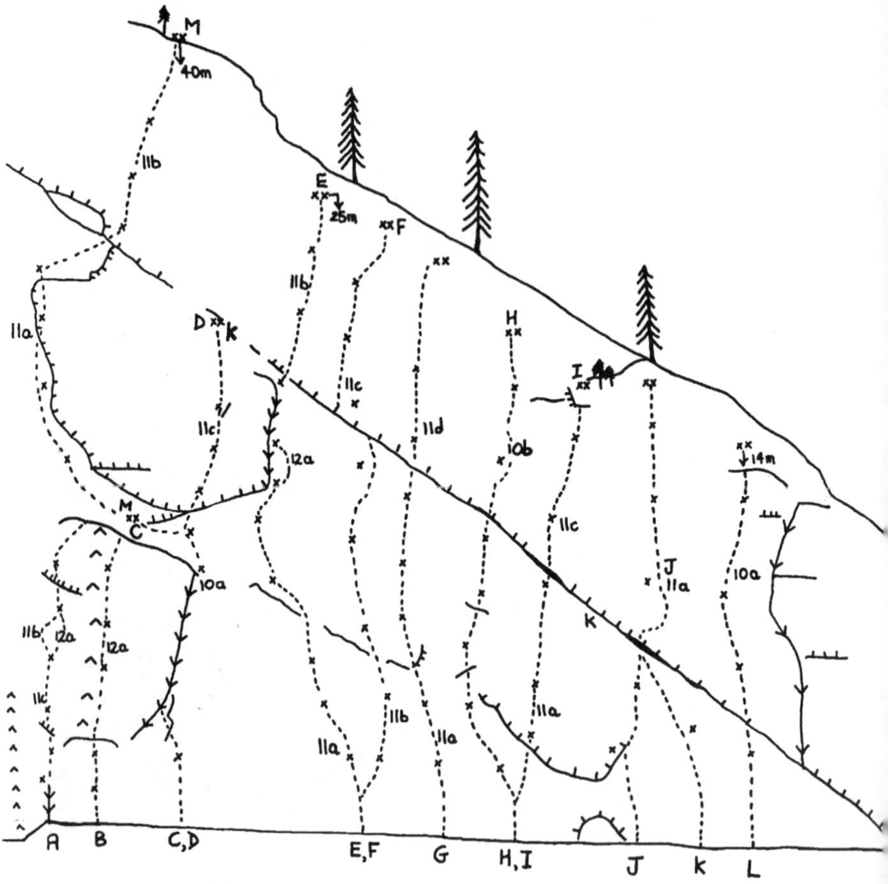


## THE ENTRANCE WALL

| | | | |
|---|---|---|---|
| A | Demonstone ** | 11c or 12a | |
| B | The Hummingbird Arete*** | 12a | |
| C | Book Worm * | 10a | nuts, 3.5 Friend |
| D | Higher Learning *** | 11c | |
| E | Open Book Exam *** | 12a | |
| F | Why Shoot the Teacher? *** | 11c | |
| G | Learning the Game ** | 11d | |
| H | Educational Process ** | 10b | |
| I | Quantum Physics ** | 11c | |
| J | Midterm ** | 11a | |
| L | Entrance Exam * | 10a | |
| K | The Accidental Tourist | 11a | TCU's, med. Friend |
| M | Advanced Education ** | 11b | |

*Jon Jones on Young Guns (11b), photo Jon Jones collection*

## WESTSIDE BUTTRESS

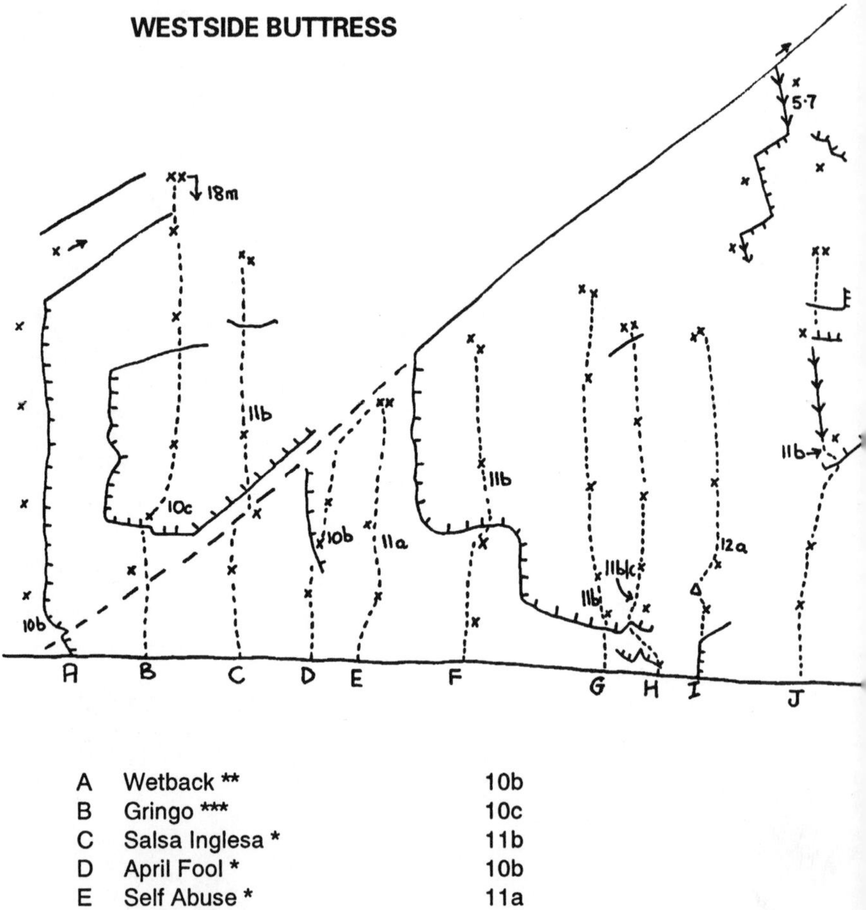


| | | |
|---|---|---|
| A | Wetback ** | 10b |
| B | Gringo *** | 10c |
| C | Salsa Inglesa * | 11b |
| D | April Fool * | 10b |
| E | Self Abuse * | 11a |
| F | Stinkfinger ** | 11b |
| G | The New Painted Lady * | 11b |
| H | Just Another John ** | 11b/c |
| I | The Fine Print * | 12a |
| J | Comfortably Numb *** | 11b |

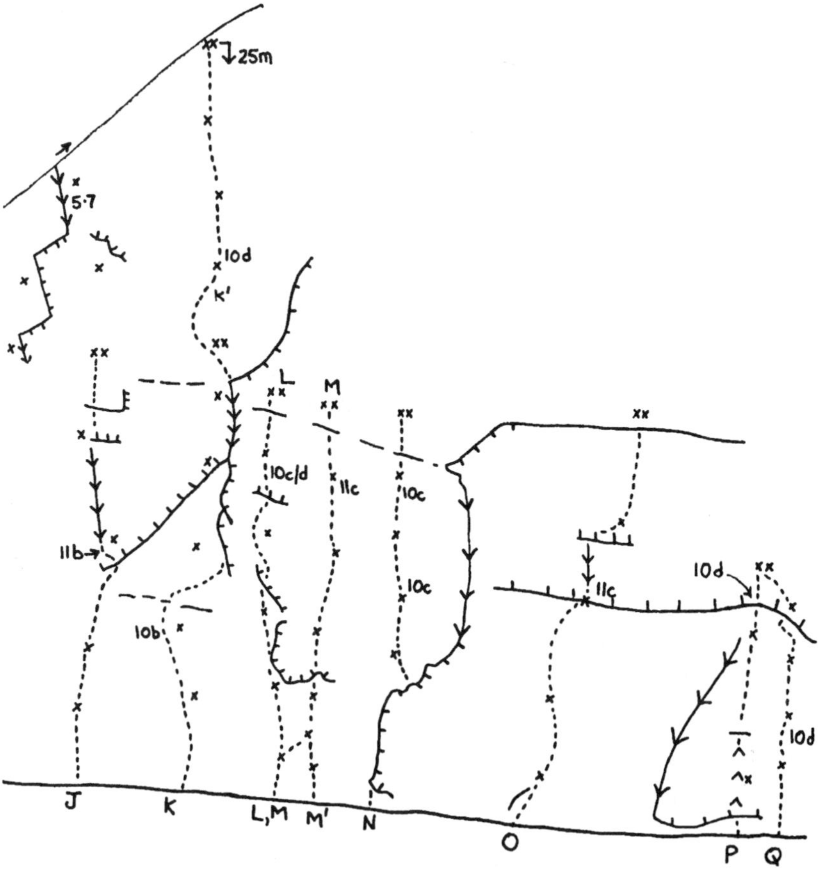


| | | |
|---|---|---|
| K | Summertime Blues (pitch 1) *** | 10b |
| K' | Summertime Blues (pitch 2) ** | 10d |
| L | Bite the Rainbow *** | 10c/d |
| M | Mistral (M' = tall person's start) ** | 11c |
| N | Scirocco *** | 10c |
| O | The Hardest 5.8 in the Rockies **** | 11c |
| P | Aquacide * | 10d |
| Q | Monkey Puzzle | 10d |

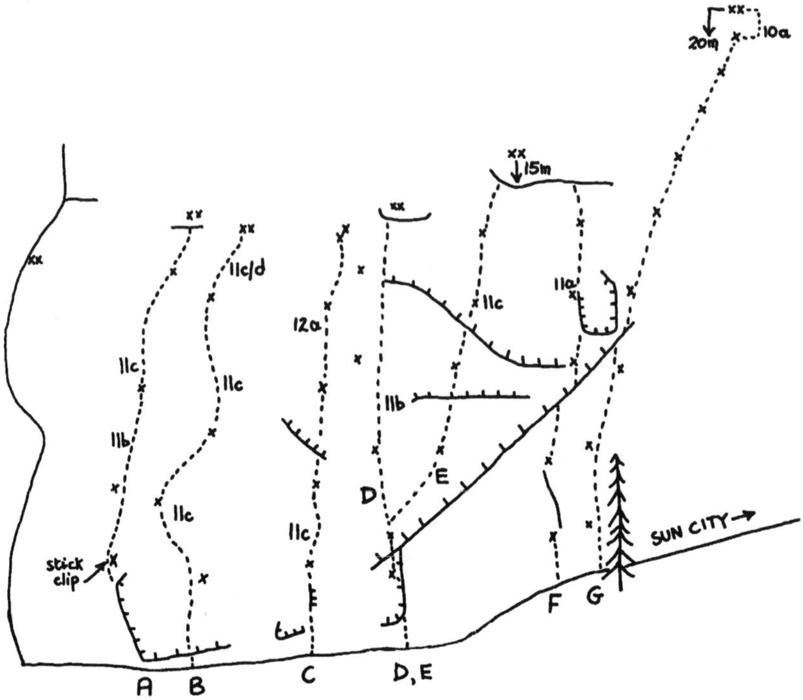


## GRAFFITI WALL

| | | |
|---|---|---|
| A | Dayglo Rage **** | 11c |
| B | Physical Graffiti **** | 11c/d |
| C | No More Mr. Nice Guy **** | 12a |
| D | Young Guns ***** | 11b |
| E | Suspended Sentence **** | 11c |
| F | The Last Word*** | 11a |
| G | American Graffiti ** | 10a |

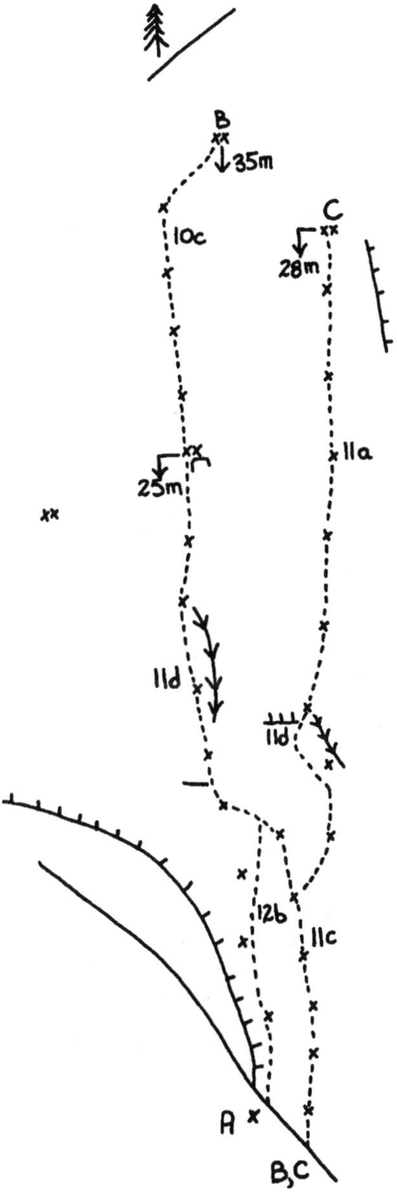


## SUN CITY

| | | |
|---|---|---|
| A | Third Degree Burn *** | 12b |
| B | Sun City *** | 11d |
| C | Sunshine Boys ** | 11d |

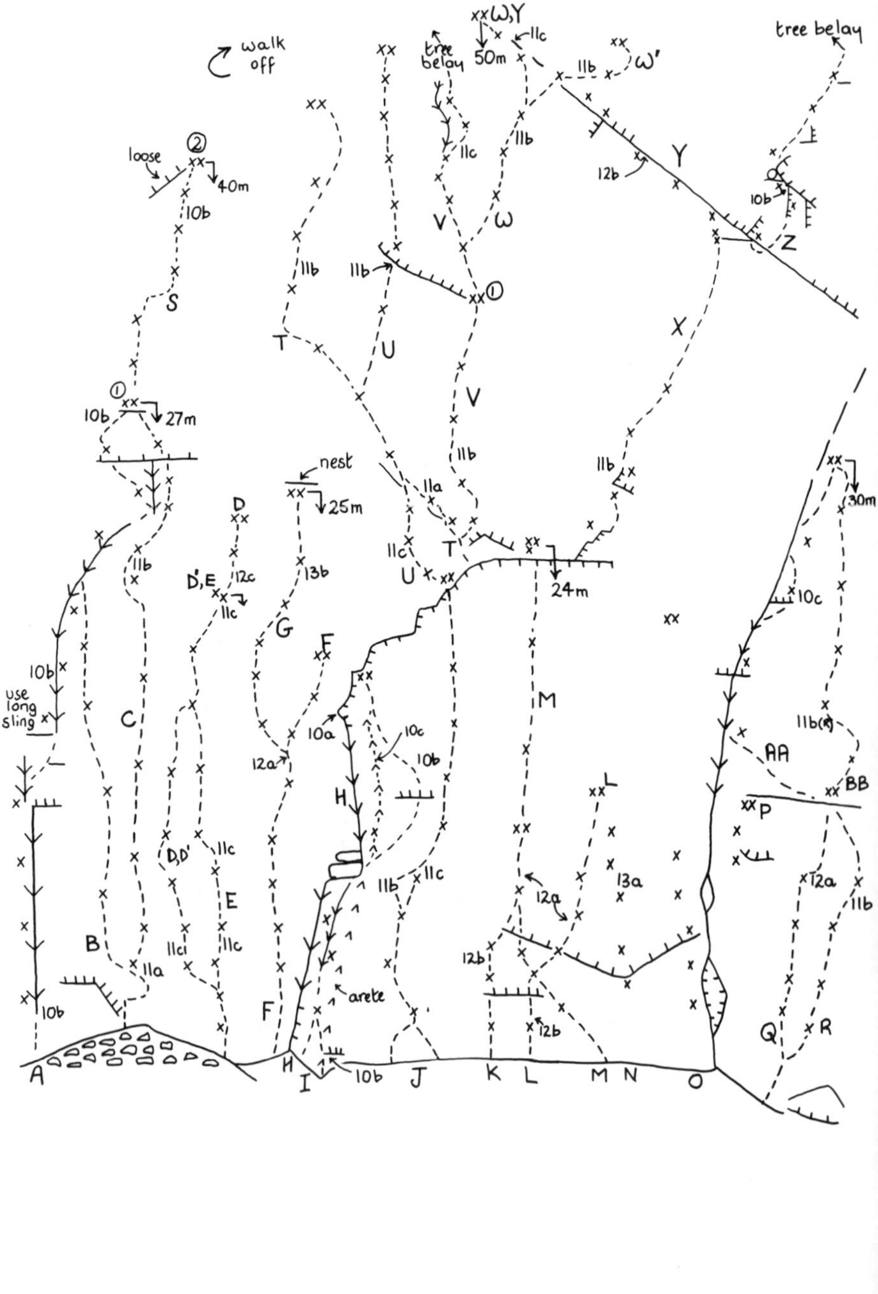

walk off
tree belay
xx W, Y
50m
11c
11b
W'
tree belay
loose
2
40m
10b
11c
11b
12b
Y
10b
Z
V
W
11b
11b
1
S
X
T
U
1
10b
27m
V
11b
11b
nest
25m
11a
D
30m
11b
12c
13b
11c
T
24m
D', E
11c
U
10c
G
F
10b
use long sling
10a
10c
M
11b(R)
AA
C
12a
10b
BB
H
L
P
D, D'
11c
12a
13a
11b
11c
11b
E
11c
11c
12a
11b
B
11a
12b
arete
12b
Q
R
10b
F
A
H
I
10b
J
K
L
M
N
O

## RAVEN'S NEST BUTTRESS

| | | | |
|---|---|---|---|
| A | Merlin's Laugh (alt. start) **** | 10b | |
| B | Merlin's Laugh (original start) **** | 11a | |
| C | The Magus *** | 11b | |
| D | The Sword in the Stone ** | 12c | |
| D' | The Short Sword *** | 11c | |
| E | Caliburn **** | 11c | |
| F | The Warlock ***** | 12a | |
| G | American Standard **** | 13b | |
| H | The Copromancer | 10a | gear to 3.5" |
| I | Coprophobia ** | 10b or c | |
| J | The Sorcerer's Apprentice **** | 11b or c | |
| K | The Lizard ** | 12b | |
| L | The Gizzard ***** | 12b | |
| M | The Wizard ***** | 12a | |
| N | project | 13a | |
| O | project | | |
| P | project | | |
| Q | Shadow of a Thin Man **** | 12a | |
| R | 110 in the Shade **** | 11b | |
| S | Merlin's Laugh (pitch 2) ** | 10b | |
| T | Witches' Brew | 11b | |
| U | The Illusionist *** | 11c | |
| V | Hocus Pocus * | 11c | best done as 2 pitches |
| W | Stolen Thunder * | 11c | |
| W' | Stolen Thunder (alt. finish) | 11b | |
| X | Prince of Darkness ** | 11b | |
| Y | Nothing Up My Sleeves ***** | 12b | |
| Z | The Enchantress ** | 10b | |
| AA | Dirty Trick | 10c | |
| BB | No Sloppy Seconds *** | 11b(R) | |

*Bill Rennie on The Wizard (12a), photo Jon Jones*

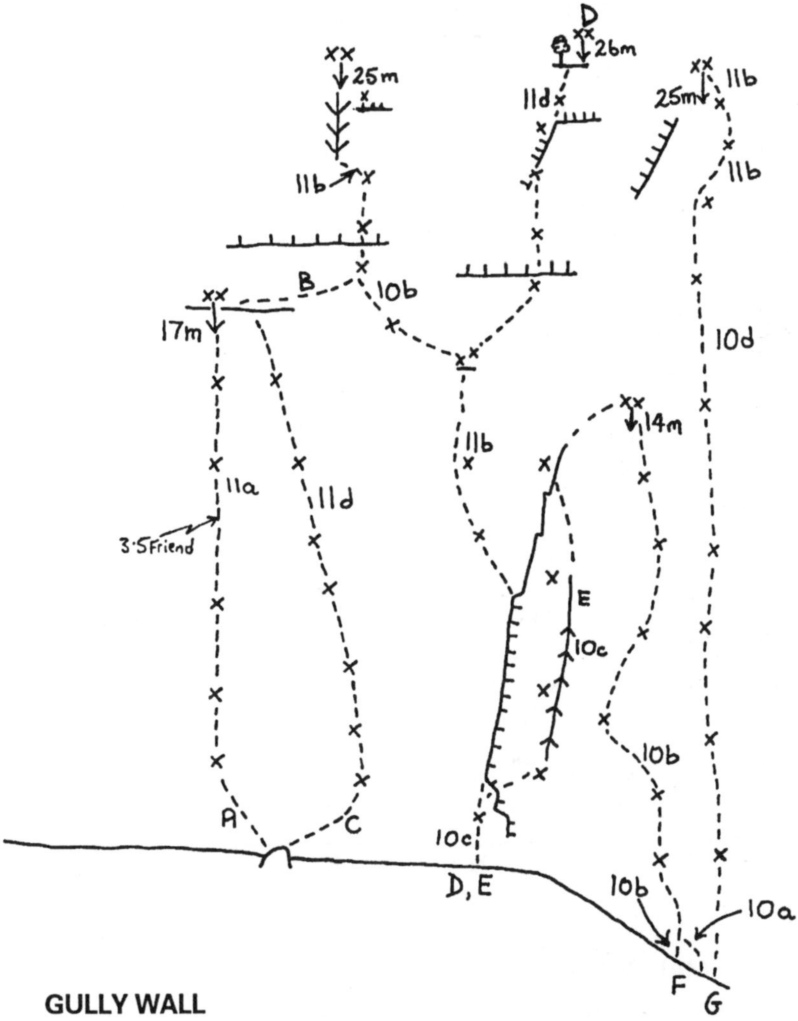


## GULLY WALL

| | | | |
|---|---|---|---|
| A | Problems With Guinness **** | 11a | 3.5 Friend |
| B | Bitter End *** | 11b | |
| C | Mephisto **** | 11d | |
| D | Abracadabra **** | 11d | nuts, Friends or use E |
| E | Sleight of Hand *** | 10c | |
| F | Hey Presto *** | 10b | |
| G | Magic in the Air *** | 11b | |

like it says small wall

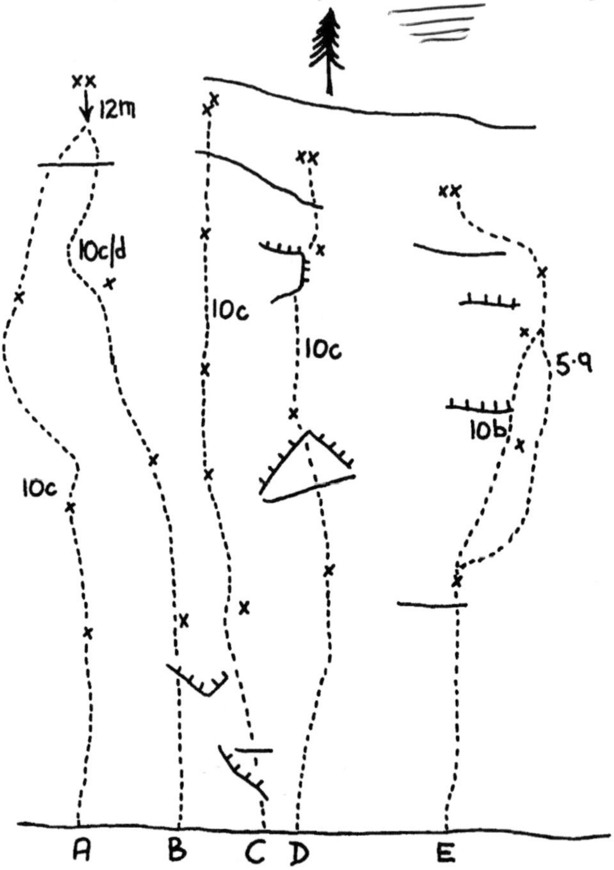


**SMALL WALL**

| | | |
|---|---|---|
| A | Small Fry | 10c |
| B | Think Tall | 10c/d |
| C | Vandals in Babylon ** | 10c |
| D | Small Is Beautiful *** | 10c |
| E | Grime and Punishment * | 5.9 |

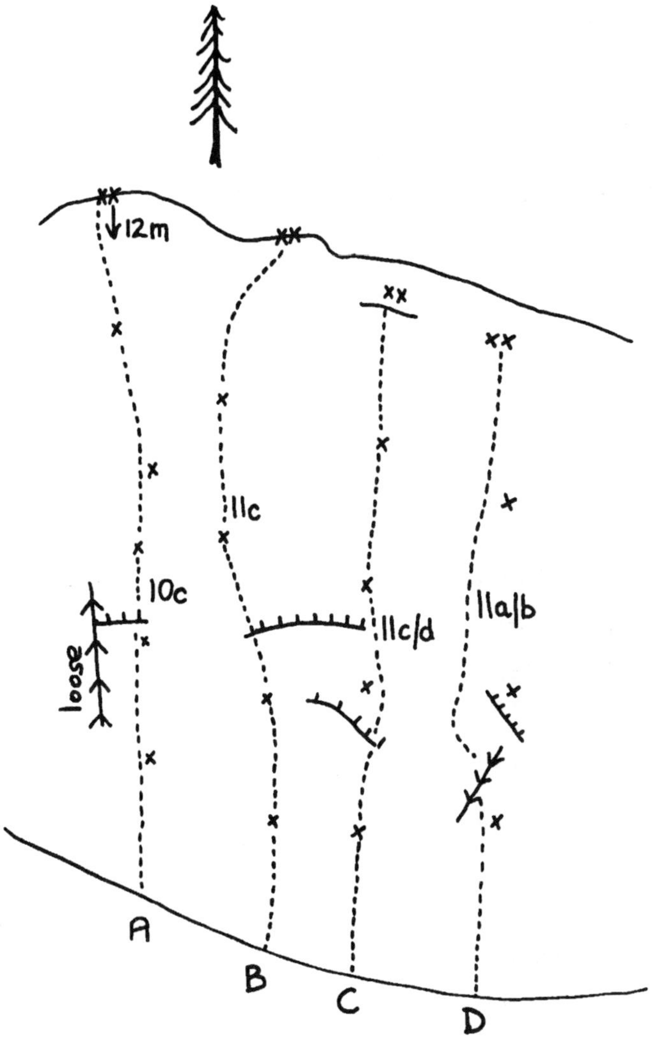


## THE WALL OF JERICHO

| | | |
|---|---|---|
| A | Equinox ** | 10c |
| B | Fall Guy * | 11c |
| C | Silent Scream ** | 11c/d |
| D | The Phoenix *** | 11a/b |

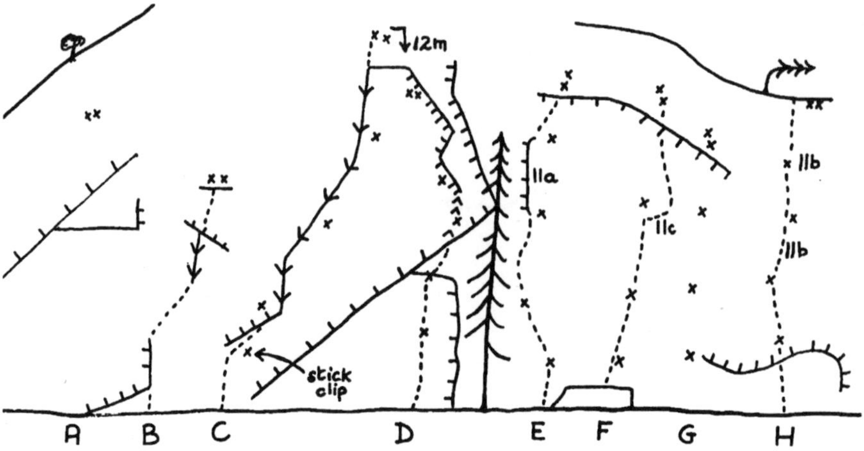


## THE EMBANKMENT

| | | |
|---|---|---|
| A | project | |
| B | project | |
| C | project | |
| D | project | |
| E | It's Not the Length That Counts *** | 11a |
| F | Digital Stimulation *** | 11c |
| G | project | |
| H | Last Gasp *** | 11b |

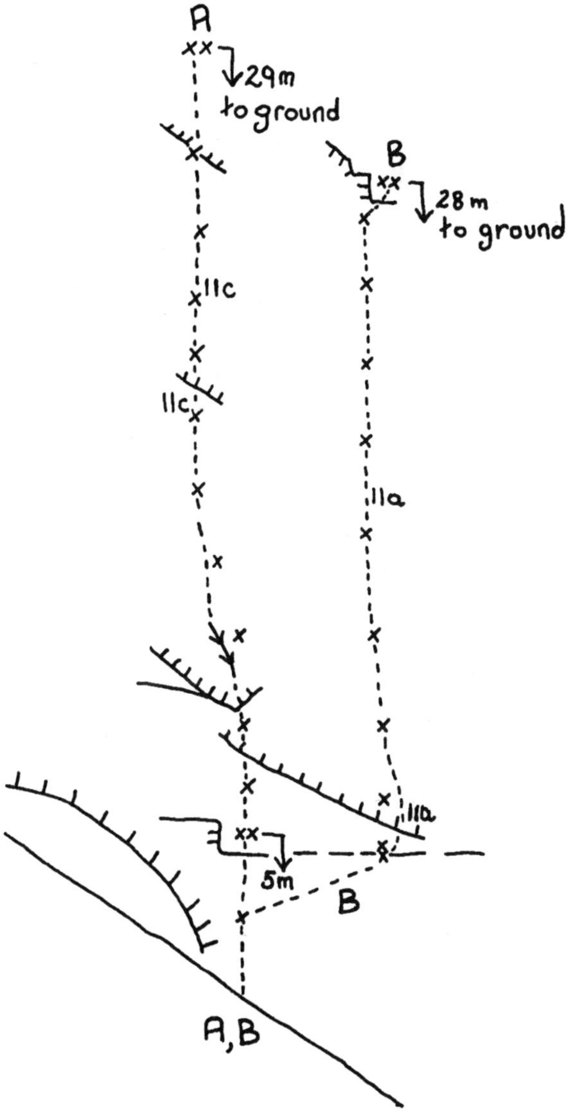


## SUMMER IN SIAM

| | | |
|---|---|---|
| A | Summer in Siam **** | 11c |
| B | Whistling in tte Dark *** | 11a |

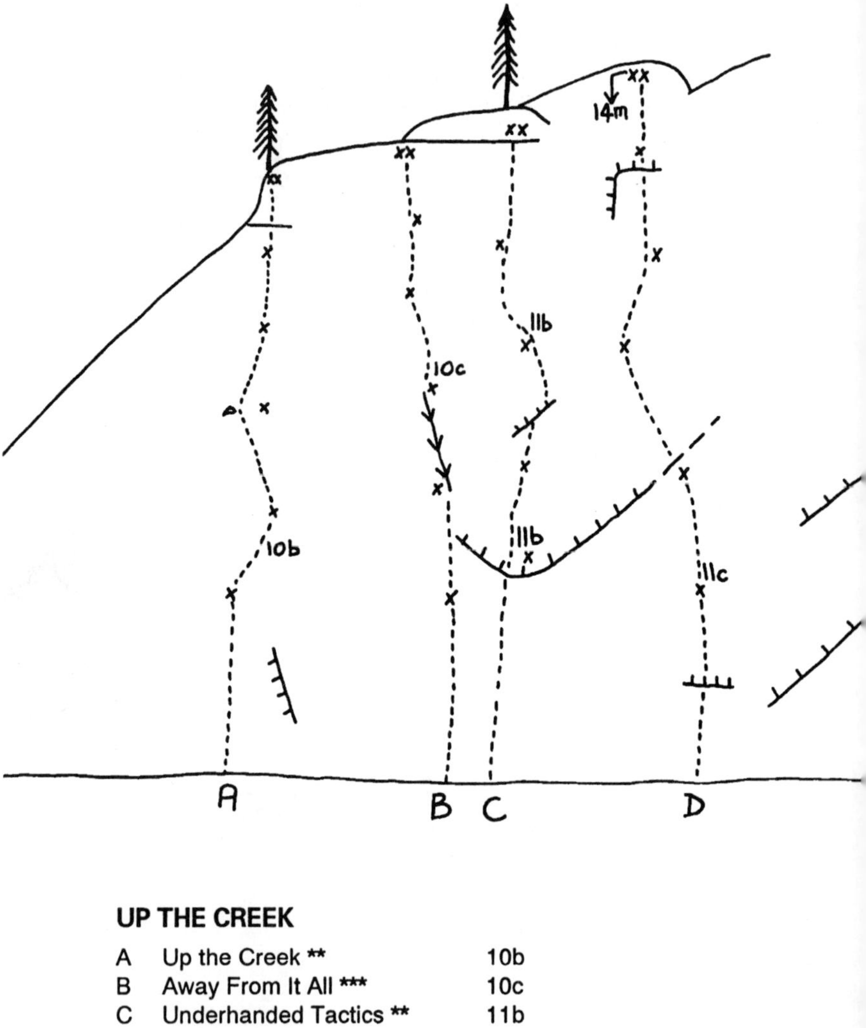


**UP THE CREEK**

| | | |
|---|---|---|
| A | Up the Creek ** | 10b |
| B | Away From It All *** | 10c |
| C | Underhanded Tactics ** | 11b |
| D | Feeling the Pinch ** | 11c |

# BATHTUB BROOK

This relatively undeveloped area is located in the drainage north of Harvie Heights (three drainages northwest of The Stoneworks). The climbs are on two cliffs: French Made Crag, a steep wall on the left (northwest) side of the creek; and Firé Wall, a steep slab across the creek from French Made Crag. All routes are fully equipped. The routes have received very few ascents and so no quality ratings are given.

**Approach**

From the Harvie Heights access road, follow Rundle Road to a small parking lot at a locked gate. Walk or bike up the gravelled continuation of the road through private land to a quarry. Bicycling is not possible beyond this point. Bypass the quarry on the right and continue up past a waterfall to gain the creek bed above. Follow the creek bed past some enjoyable slickrock scrambling, eventually reaching the cliffs in about 45 minutes from Harvie Heights. The approach is difficult except in dry weather when the creek is low.

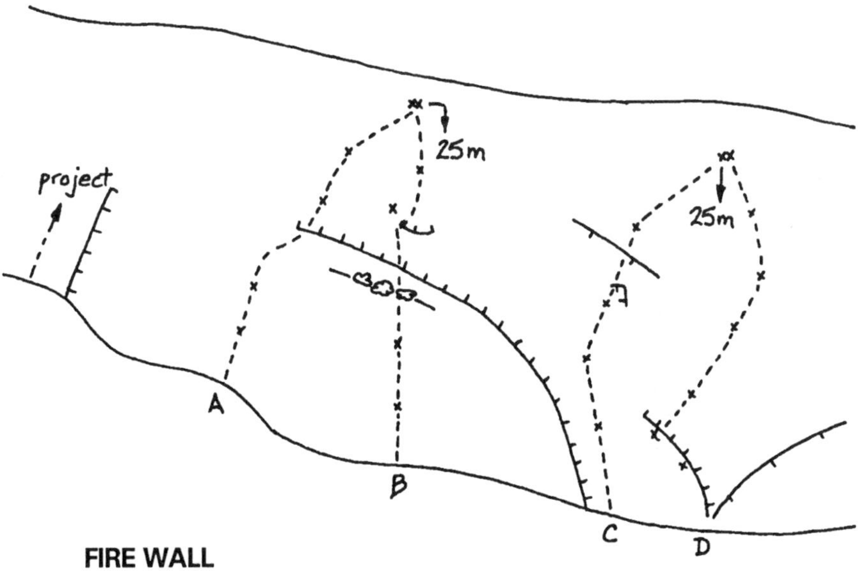


**FIRE WALL**

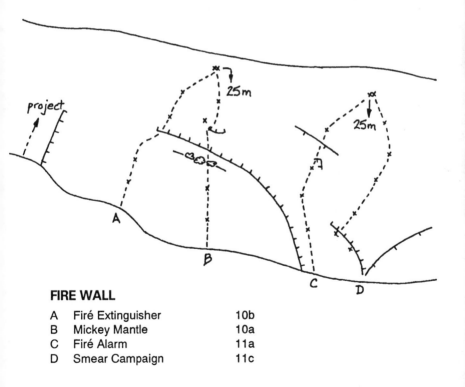

| | | |
|---|---|---|
| A | Firé Extinguisher | 10b |
| B | Mickey Mantle | 10a |
| C | Firé Alarm | 11a |
| D | Smear Campaign | 11c |

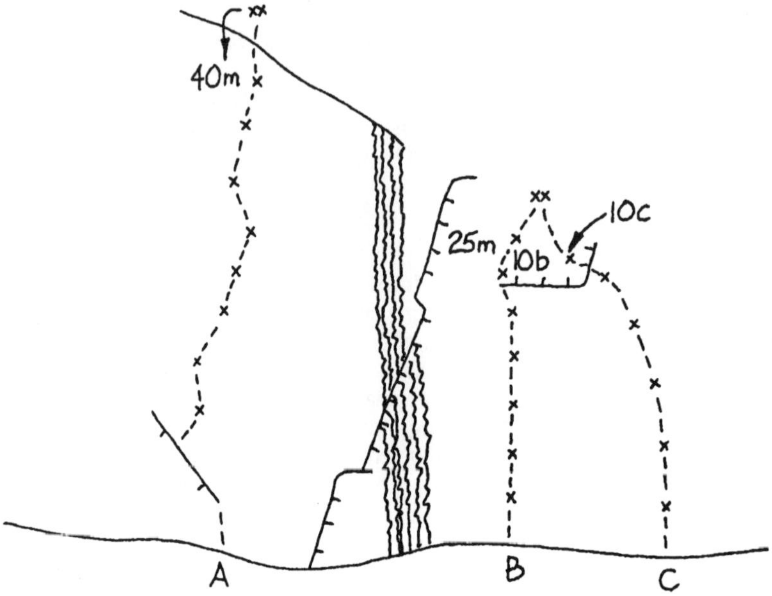


**FRENCH MADE CRAG**

| | | |
|---|---|---|
| A | French Made | 10b |
| B | Hotwire ** | 10b |
| C | Madame X * | 10c |

# THE STONEWORKS

The Stoneworks is located in the drainage left (northwest) of Mt Lady MacDonald. The main climbing area is a narrow, twisting, water-smoothed canyon, called the Lower Canyon. Other routes are found on two cliffs a short distance beyond the top end of the canyon: Weird Wall, a short, south facing cliff; and The Arcade, a large, north-facing wall. Sport climbing is the rule here: all climbs are protected entirely by bolts and have chained, two-bolt rappel anchors. The routes are relatively short and can nearly all be descended using one rope. Wait for warm weather to climb here — most of the routes see little or no sun.

**Approach**

From the Trans Canada Highway, take the west Canmore exit and drive east along the service road that parallels the Trans Canada on the north side. The service road is also accessible by turning west from Benchlands Trail, which crosses the Trans Canada farther east at an overpass. Park at a gate approximately opposite the Shell station across the highway. The gate is at the crest of a hill, 1.3 km from the west Canmore exit and 2 km from Benchlands Trail. Cross the fence and walk up a short, steep paved road into a clearing. The drainage is ahead and slightly left. Follow trails and abandoned roads, reclosing any gates you go through, until the valley narrows and you are forced into the creek bed. It is possible to bicycle to this point. Continue up the creek bed to the canyon — a pleasant 45 minutes or so from the parking spot. To reach Weird Wall, walk up the creek bed a couple of minutes beyond the top end of the canyon until you reach a small cliff on the left, just a few metres above the valley bottom. This point also marks the start of the trail to The Arcade, which heads up right through boulders and scree to reach the cliff at *Tempest.*

***DO NOT ATTEMPT TO GET TO THE ARCADE DIRECTLY FROM THE HEAD OF THE CANYON BY FOLLOWING ALONG THE BASE OF THE CLIFFS.*** This slope is easily eroded and is littered with large unstable boulders; furthermore, it doesn't save any time to go that way.

The initial portion of the approach may change in the near future with construction of the Hyatt Regency Hotel.

*Bill Rennie on Penguin Lust (10b), photo Jon Jones*

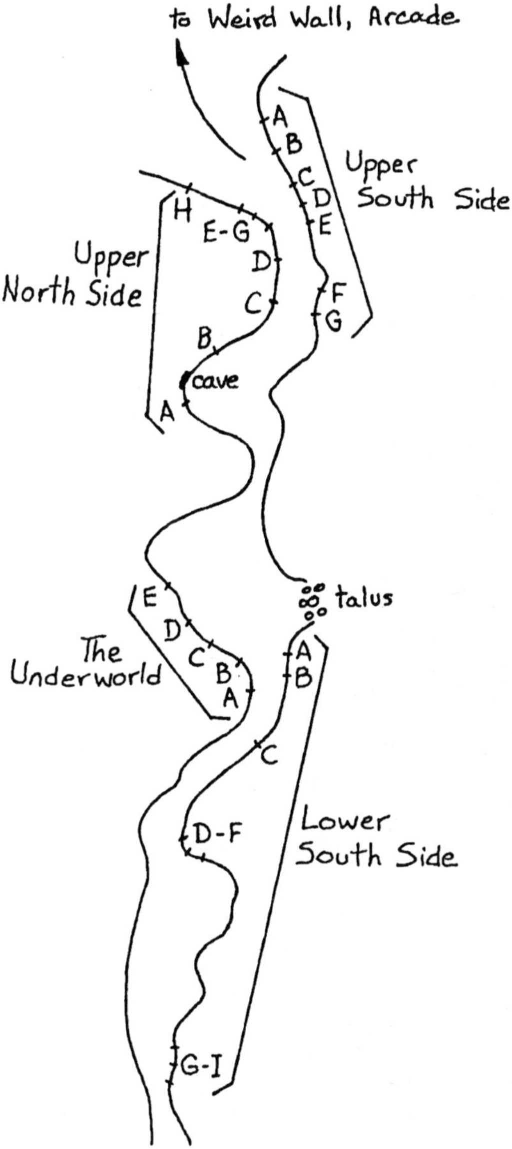
to Weird Wall, Arcade
A
B
C
D
E
F
G
Upper South Side
H
E-G
D
C
B
cave
A
Upper North Side
talus
E
D
C
B
A
The Underworld
A
B
C
D-F
G-I
Lower South Side

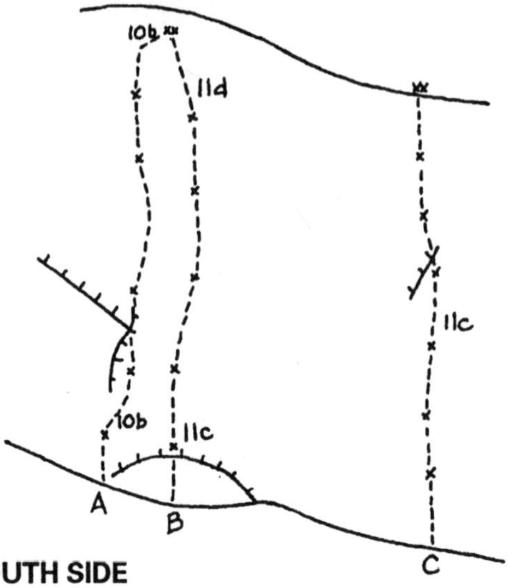


**LOWER SOUTH SIDE**

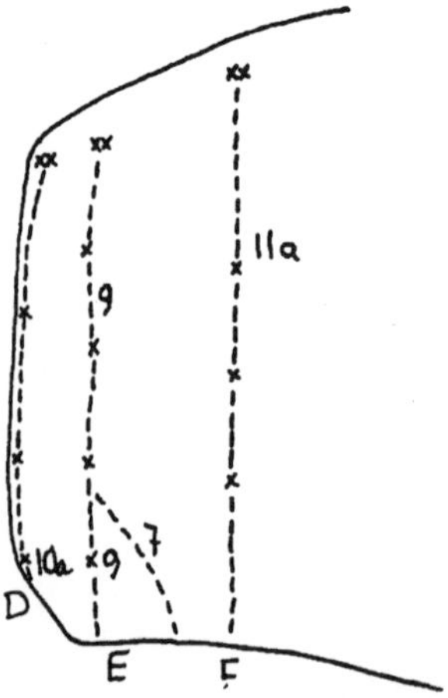


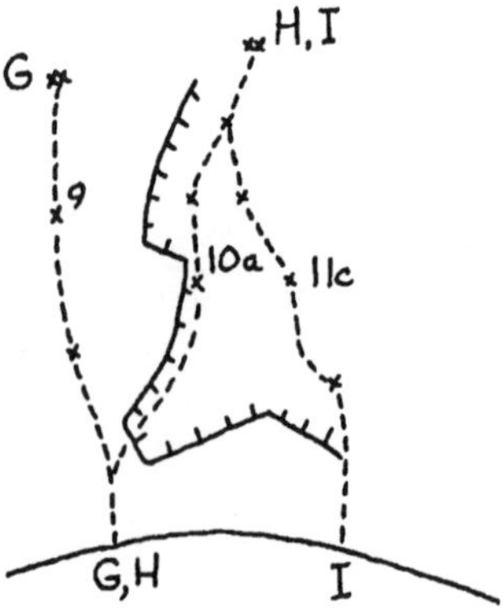


| | | |
|---|---|---|
| A | So It's a Sport Climb **** | 10b |
| B | Wings of Desire ** | 11d |
| C | Spider in a Tub *** | 11c |
| D | Kali** | 10a |
| E | Loki ** | 9 |
| F | Runners on 'Roids ** | 11a |
| G | Girl Muscles * | 9 |
| H | Clip Trip ** | 10a |
| I | Power Hour *** | 11c |

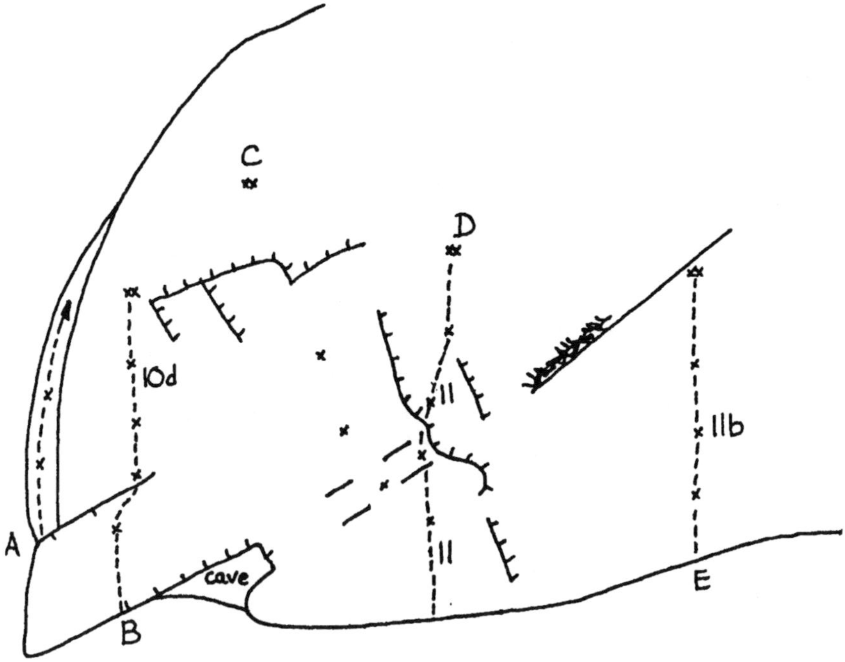


**THE UNDERWORLD**

| | | |
|---|---|---|
| A | The Access Line | 9 |
| B | Wise Guys **** | 10d |
| C | project | |
| D | Capone **** | 11b |
| E | Younger Than Yesterday ** | 11b |

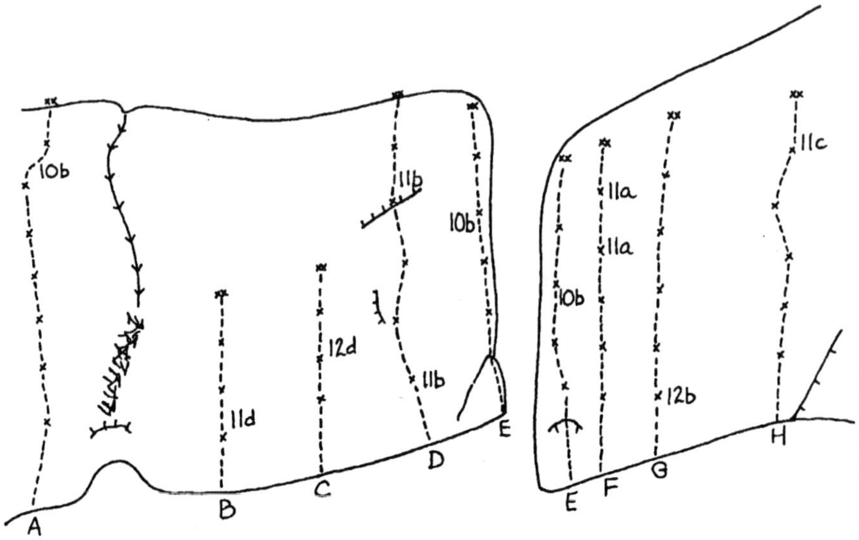


## UPPER NORTH SIDE

| | | | |
|---|---|---|---|
| A | Cro Magnon *** | 10b | |
| B | Klingon War ** | 11c/d | |
| C | Slap Shot | 12d | toprope |
| D | Hat Trick *** | 11b | |
| E | Penguin Lust **** | 10b | |
| F | Electric Ocean ***** | 11a | |
| G | Blue Lotus ** | 12b | |
| H | Love and Death | 11c | |

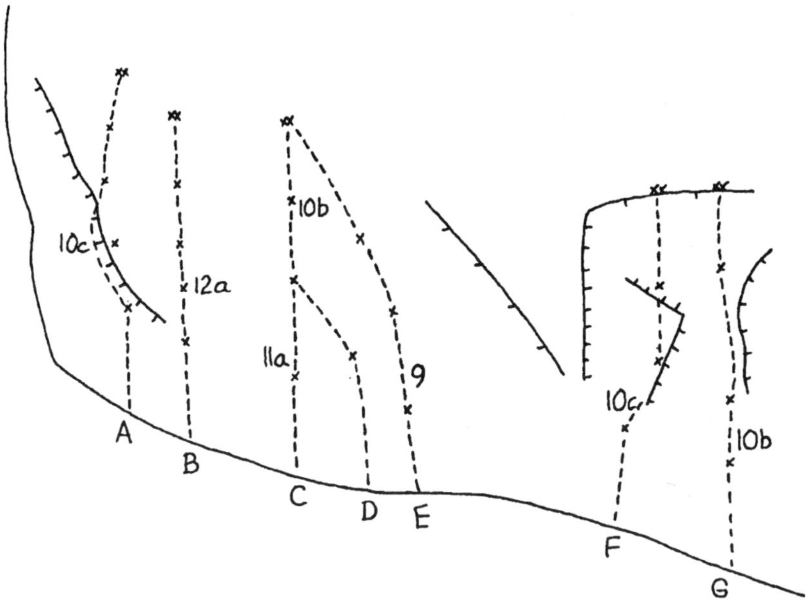


## UPPER SOUTH SIDE

| | | |
|---|---|---|
| A | Under the Gun **** | 10c |
| B | Brent's Big Birthday ** | 12a/b |
| C | Holey Redeemer Direct ** | 11a |
| D | Holey Redeemer *** | 10b |
| E | Baby Buoux * | 9 |
| F | Junior Woodchuck Jamboree ** | 10c |
| G | Boy Scout Fundraiser * | 10b |

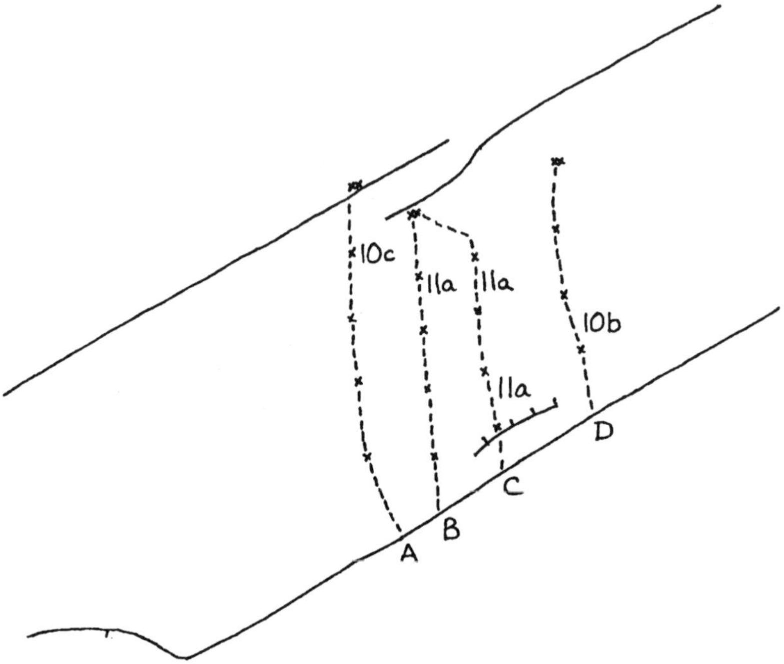


## WEIRD WALL

| | | |
|---|---|---|
| A | When the Going Gets Weird *** | 10c |
| B | The Weird Turn Pro *** | 11a |
| C | Gravity Rodeo *** | 11a/b |
| D | Weird Noises ** | 10b |

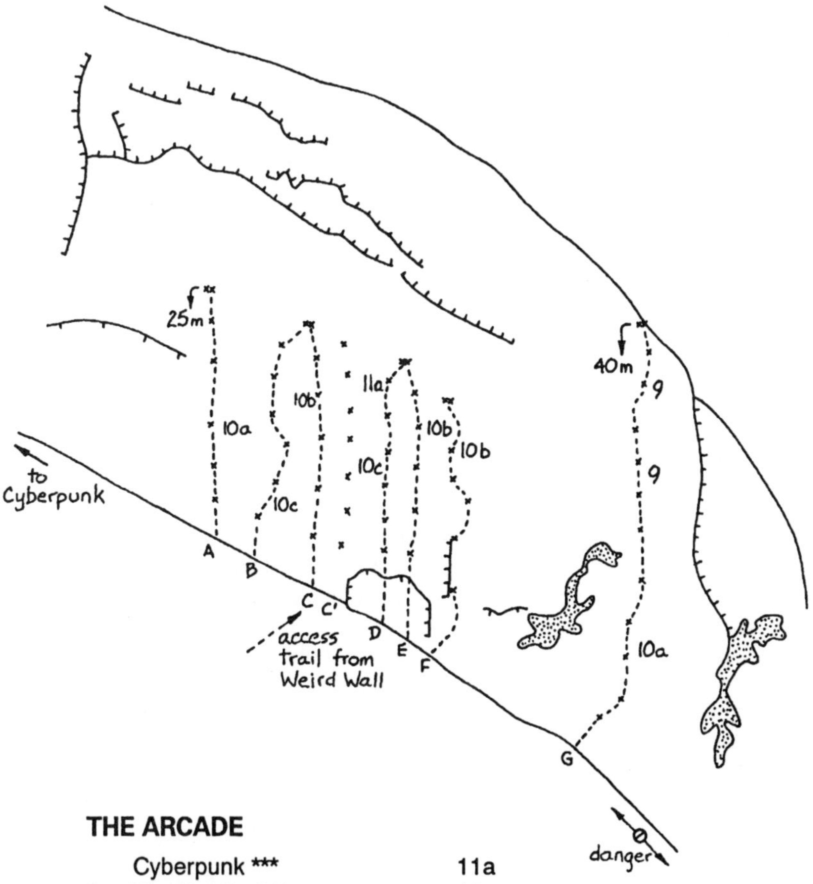


## THE ARCADE

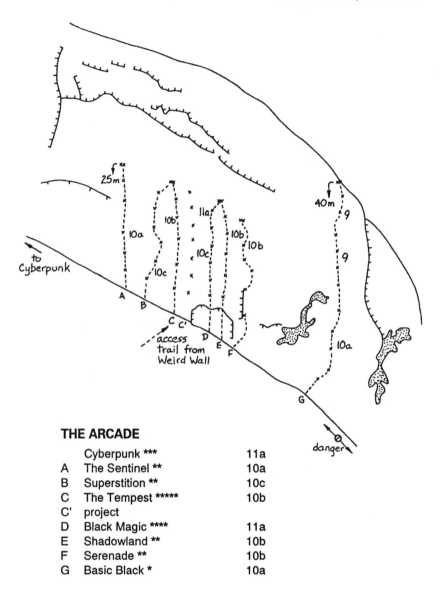

| | | |
|---|---|---|
| | Cyberpunk *** | 11a |
| A | The Sentinel ** | 10a |
| B | Superstition ** | 10c |
| C | The Tempest ***** | 10b |
| C' | project | |
| D | Black Magic **** | 11a |
| E | Shadowland ** | 10b |
| F | Serenade ** | 10b |
| G | Basic Black * | 10a |

# COUGAR CANYON

Cougar Canyon is the prominent drainage immediately northeast of Canmore, between Mt Lady MacDonald and Grotto Mountain. Virtually all of the routes are fully equipped. As in all the canyons, chasing the sun becomes a major preoccupation on cool spring and fall days. The right side of House of Cards is the warmest morning crag in the canyon, catching full sun on even the shortest days. Other good morning areas are Catseye Cliff (especially the upper end), Catamount Crag, Cosmology Crag, Canadian Forks and Creekside Crag. The best afternoon sun is at Covert Crag and Crowbar Crag; Chameleon Cliff and Made in the Shade come into the sun on summer evenings. Although most of the climbs are short, several require two ropes to descend.

**Approach**

From the east: take Elk Run Boulevard, which leads north from Highway 1A about 500 metres east of the Trans Canada Highway interchange (the east entrance to Canmore). After about 1 km, Elk Run Boulevard crosses Cougar Creek at the top of a gradual hill. From the west, the same point is reached by taking Benchlands Trail, which crosses the Trans Canada Highway by way of an overpass. The parking situation has changed several times during the last two years, and may do so again. At the time of writing, cars must be parked on the pavement (avoid the no parking signs at the curve) rather than in the obvious gravel area to the north. Walk or bike up a gravel road on the west side of the creek for about 1 km, then continue up a good trail. There are several creek crossings but it is easy to keep your feet dry except when the water is high. Total walking time to the first climbing, at House of Cards Cliff, is about 15 to 20 minutes; Cosmology Crag is about 15 minutes farther; and Canadian Forks and Creekside Crag are a scenic 20 to 25 minutes more. It is possible, but hardly worth the effort, to bicycle as far as Creekside Crag.

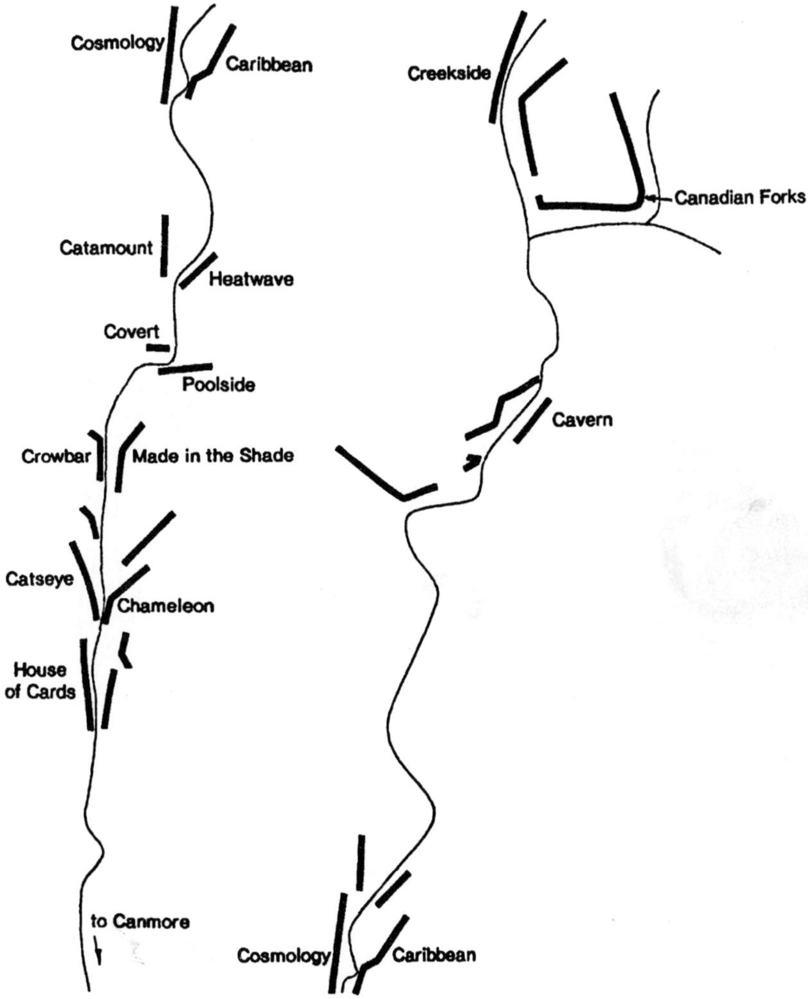
Cosmology
Caribbean
Creekside
Canadian Forks
Catamount
Heatwave
Covert
Poolside
Cavern
Crowbar
Made in the Shade
Catseye
Chameleon
House
of Cards
to Canmore
Cosmology
Caribbean

## HOUSE OF CARDS, LEFT

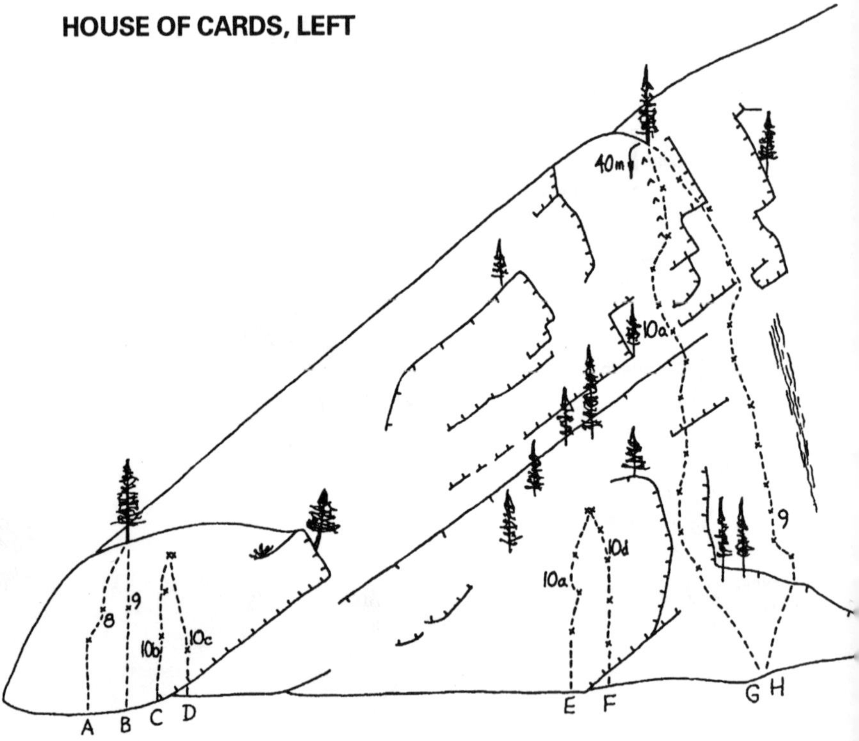


| | | |
|---|---|---|
| A | Rock 101 * | 8 Lead |
| B | Empty Nest | 9 |
| C | Rock 201 * | 10b |
| D | Breathless ** | 10c |
| E | Innuendo | 10a |
| F | Fly By Wire * | 10d/11a |
| G | Solarium * | 10a |
| H | Aqualung ** | 9/10a |

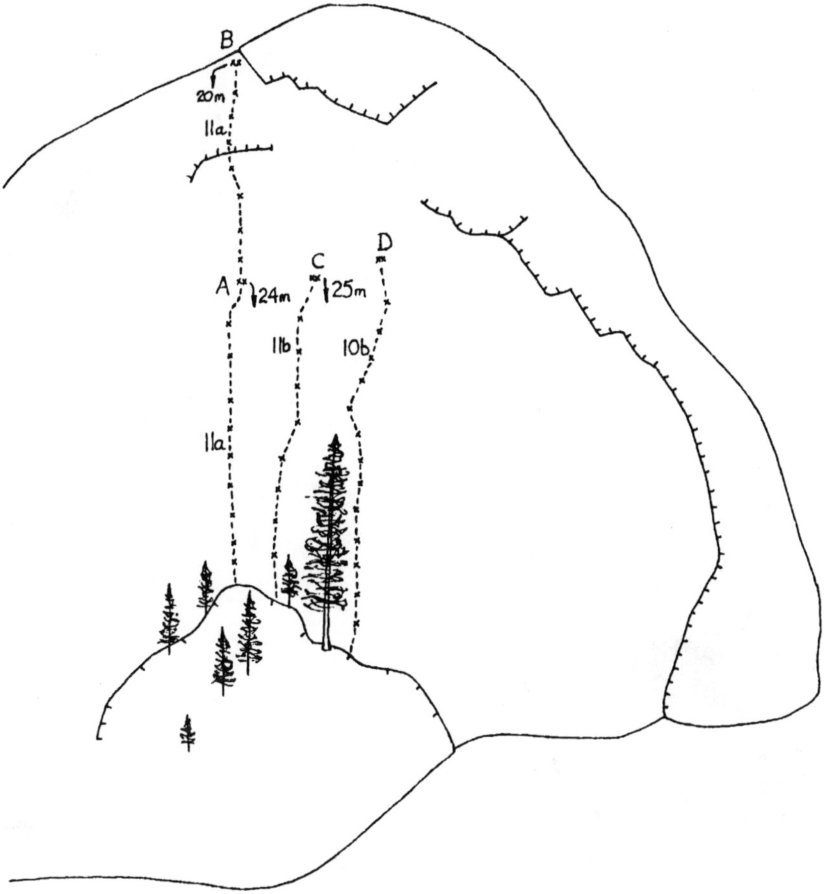


## HOUSE OF CARDS, RIGHT

| | | |
|---|---|---|
| A | Ashtaroth *** | 11a |
| B | Heliopolis *** | 11a |
| C | Is That Your 'Dog? ** | 11b |
| D | Byzantium **** | 10b |

John Martin on Byzantium (10b), photo Jon Jones

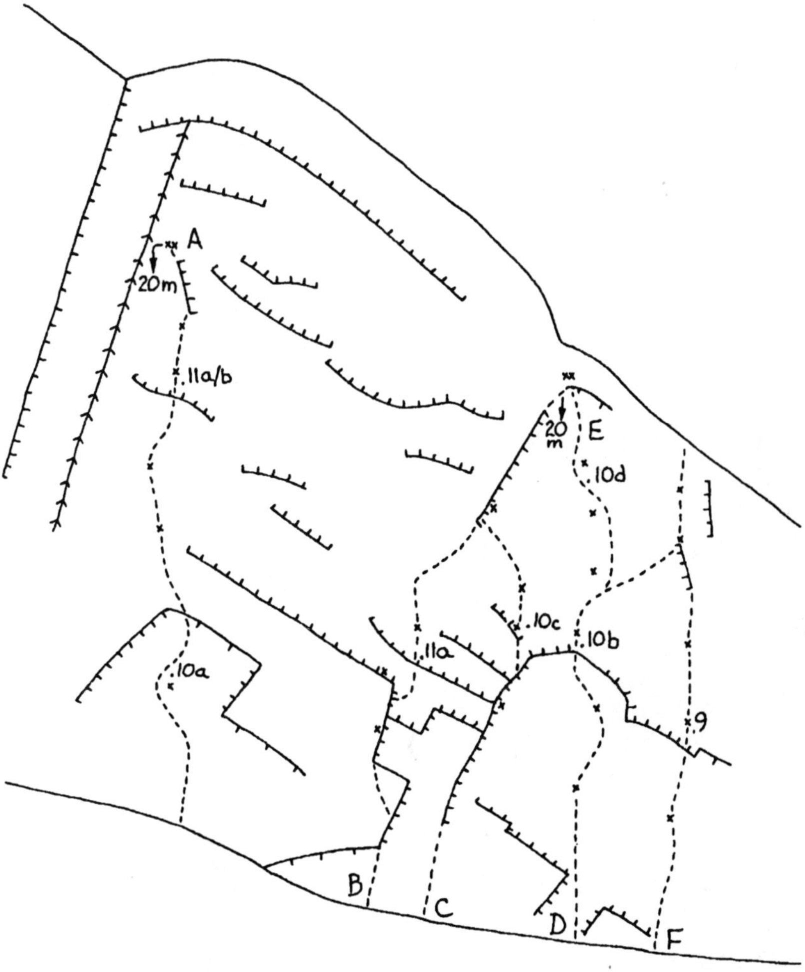


## CHAMELEON CLIFF

| | | |
|---|---|---|
| A | Faux Pas *** | 11a/b |
| B | Cold Shoulder | 11a |
| C | Chameleon * | 10c |
| D | Thrushold ** | 10b |
| E | Thrushold Direct ** | 10d |
| F | Call of the Wild * | 9 |

## CATSEYE CLIFF, LEFT

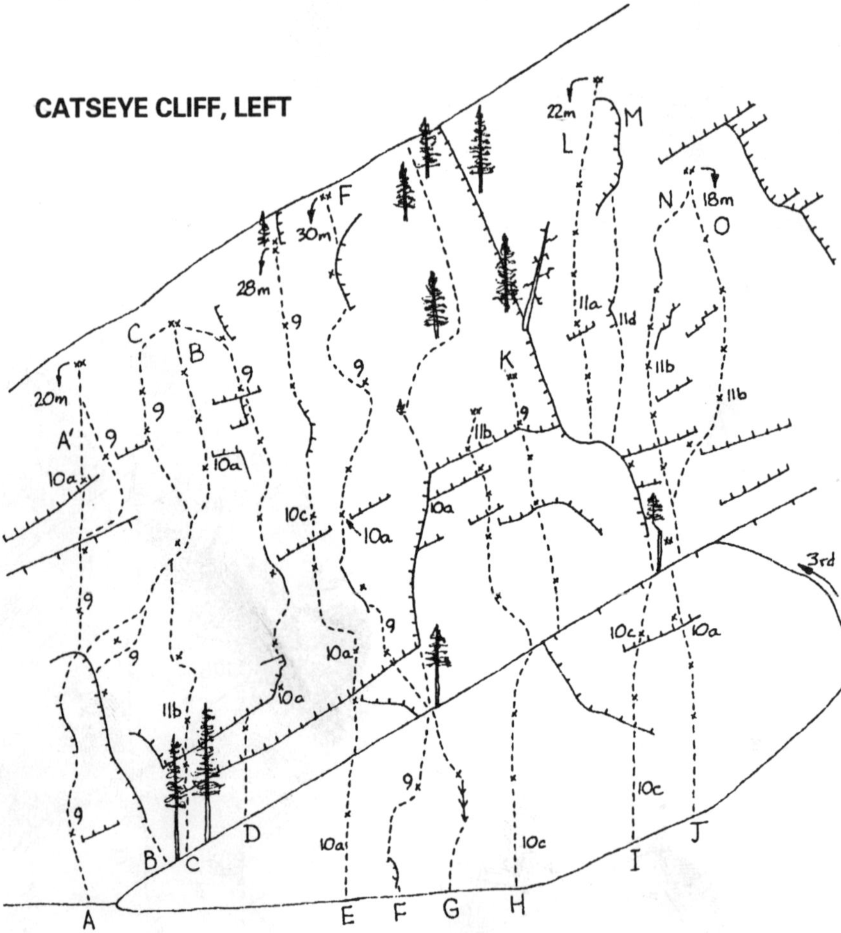


| | | | |
|---|---|---|---|
| A | Catspaw ** | 9 | |
| A' | Catspaw Direct * | 10a | |
| B | Catseye ** | 10a | |
| C | Dr Tongue's 3D House of Slave Chicks** | 11b/c | |
| D | Double Header *** | 10a | |
| E | Coconut Joe * | 10c | |
| F | Banana Republic * | 10a | |
| G | Temerity | 10a | not recommended |
| H | Rough Trade ** | 11b | |
| I | Lapidarist | 10c | |
| J | Impulse * | 10a | |
| K | Swan Lake | 9/10a | |
| L | Dressed to Kill *** | 11a/b | |
| M | Repulse | 11d | toprope |
| N | Wilt **** | 11b | |

## CATSEYE CLIFF, RIGHT

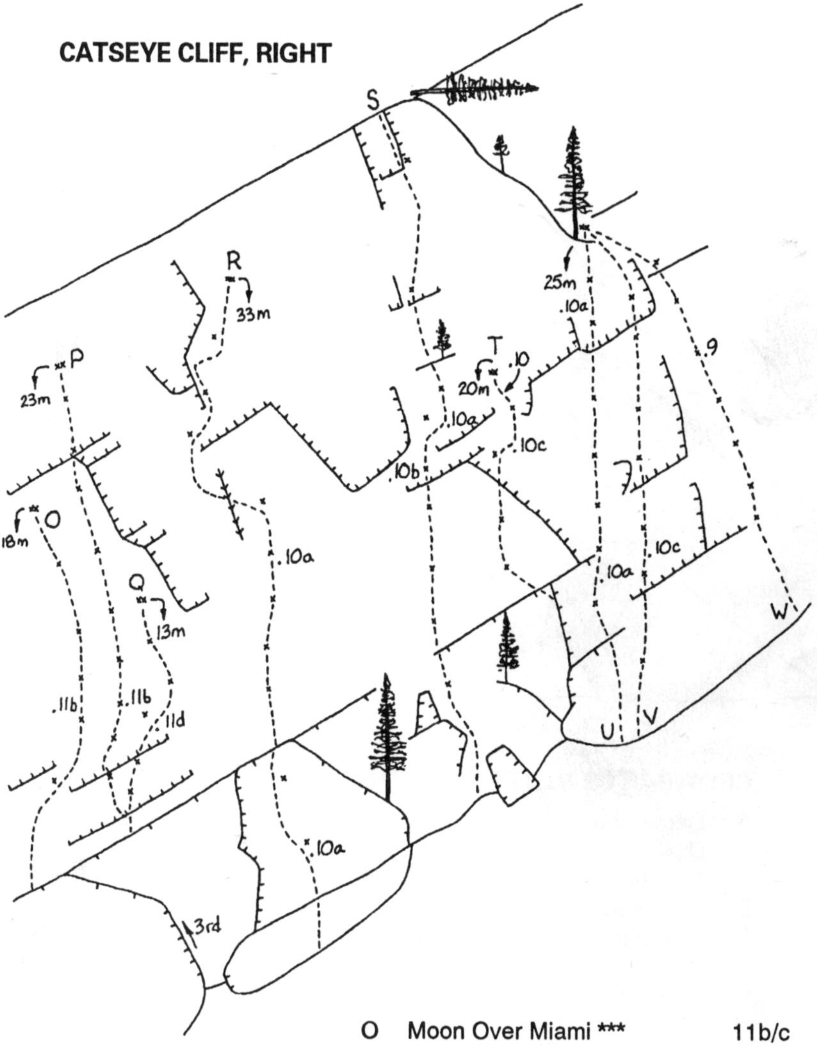

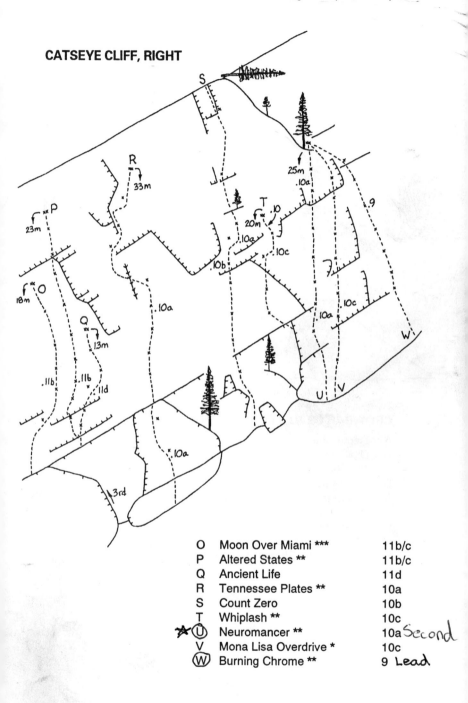

| | | |
|---|---|---|
| O | Moon Over Miami *** | 11b/c |
| P | Altered States ** | 11b/c |
| Q | Ancient Life | 11d |
| R | Tennessee Plates ** | 10a |
| S | Count Zero | 10b |
| T | Whiplash ** | 10c |
| ★ Ⓤ | Neuromancer ** | 10a Second |
| V | Mona Lisa Overdrive * | 10c |
| Ⓦ | Burning Chrome ** | 9 Lead |

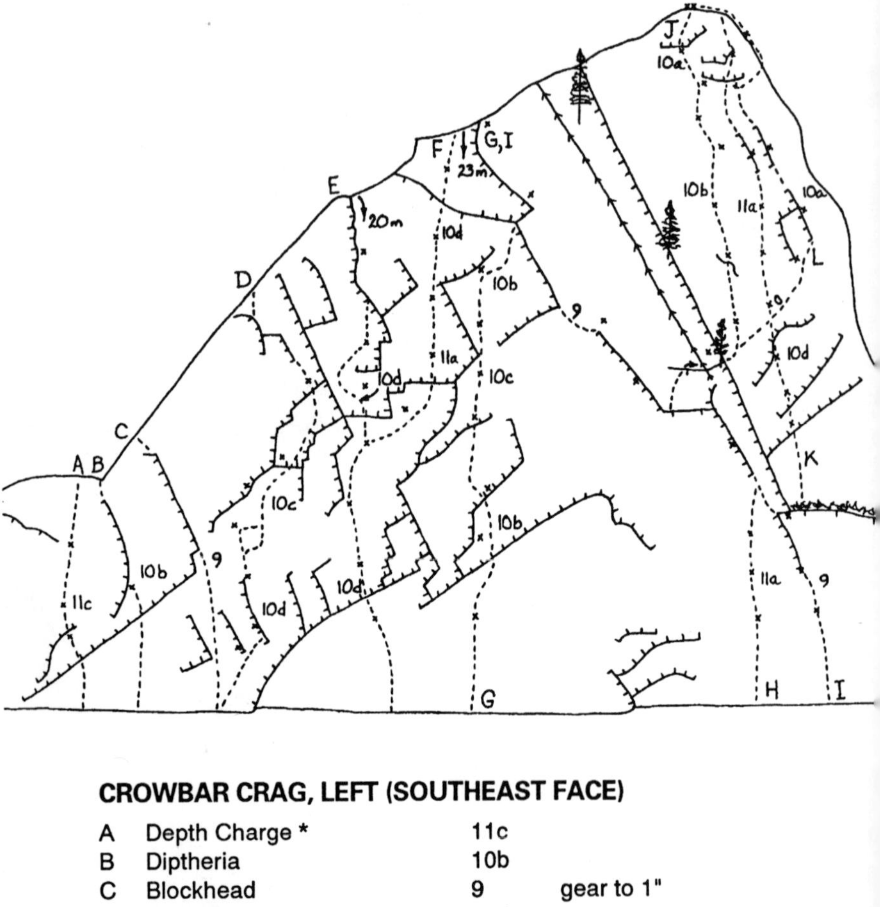


## CROWBAR CRAG, LEFT (SOUTHEAST FACE)

| | | | |
|---|---|---|---|
| A | Depth Charge * | 11c | |
| B | Diptheria | 10b | |
| C | Blockhead | 9 | gear to 1" |
| D | Block Buster *** | 10d | |
| E | Shockwave **** | 10d | |
| F | Surface Tension ** | 11a/b | |
| G | Critical Mass**** | 10c | |
| H | Island Experience * | 11a | |
| I | Islands in the Stream ** | 9 | |
| J | Face Value **** | 10b | |
| K | Mean Street ** | 11a | |
| L | Argon ** | 10a | |

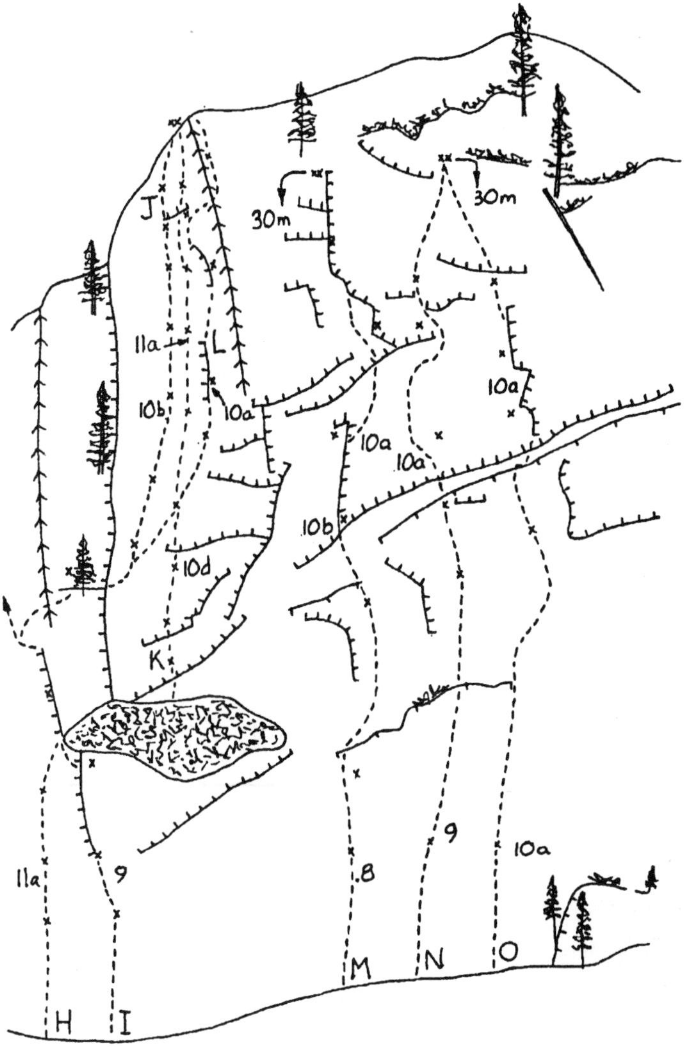


## CROWBAR CRAG, RIGHT (NORTHEAST FACE)

| | | |
|---|---|---|
| H | Island Experience * | 11a |
| I | Islands in the Stream ** | 9 |
| J | Face Value **** | 10b |
| K | Mean Street ** | 11a |
| L | Argon ** | 10a |
| M | Jack of Clubs * | 10b |
| N | Sleeping Dog ** | 10a |
| O | Slow Turning ** | 10a |

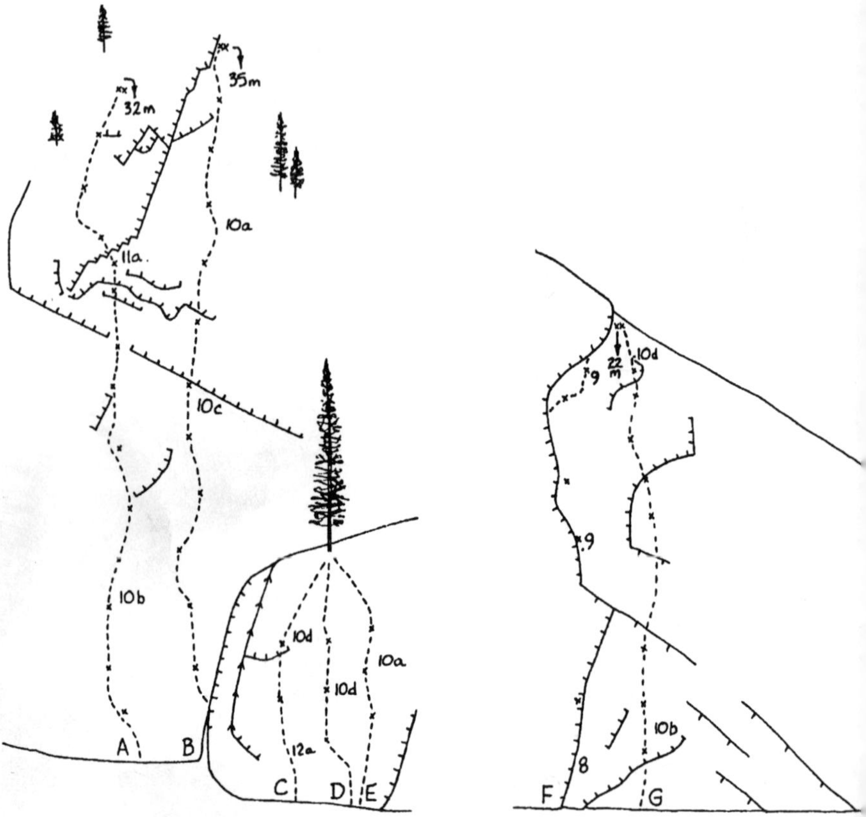


## MADE IN THE SHADE

| | | |
|---|---|---|
| A | Tender Mercies ** | 11a |
| B | Made in the Shade *** | 10c |
| C | French Connection * | 12a |
| D | Tree Men **** | 10d |
| E | Crybaby ** | 10a |
| F | Turning Shadows *** | 9 Lead |
| G | High Wire * | 10d |

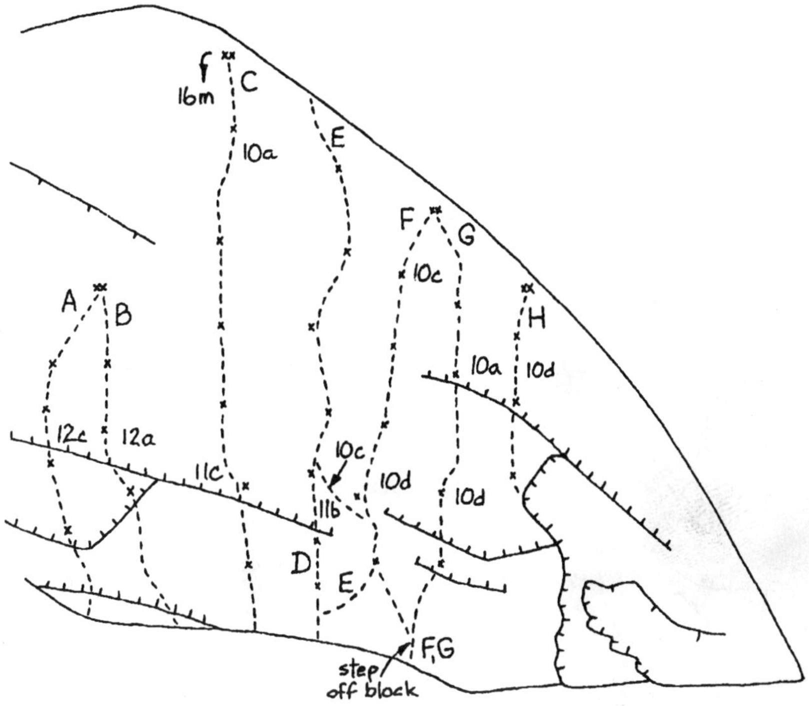


## POOLSIDE CRAG

| | | | |
|---|---|---|---|
| A | Stygian Ayre *** | 12c | |
| B | Chandelle ** | 12a | |
| C | Dark Star *** | 11c | |
| D | Bob's Direct *** | 11b | |
| E | Bob's Yer Uncle *** | 10c | |
| F | Party Line *** | 10d | |
| G | Poolside Pleasures **** | 10d | |
| H | Diving Board, The *** | 10d | optional Friend 2-2.5 |

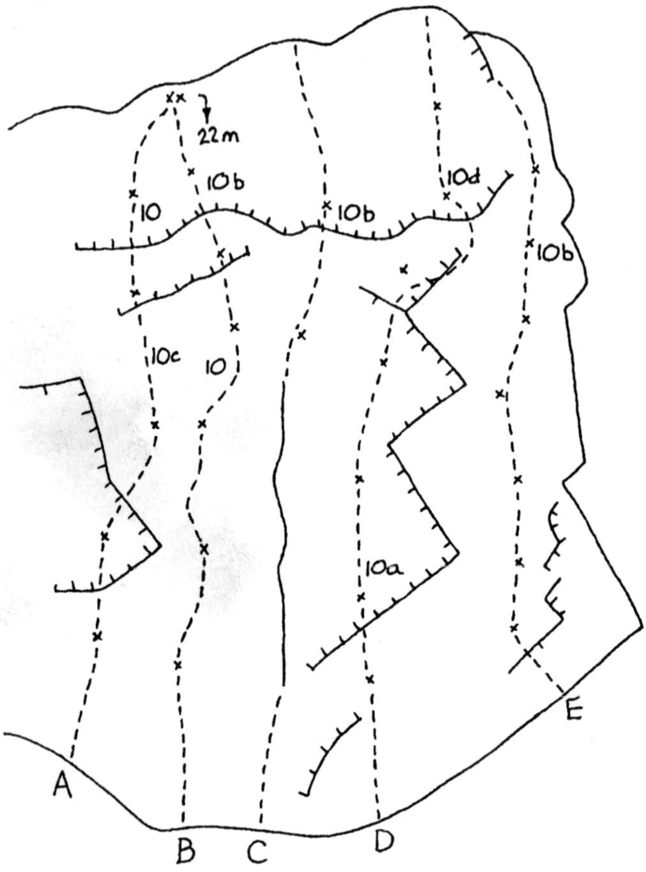


**COVERT CRAG**

| | | | |
|---|---|---|---|
| A | Cloak and Dagger ** | 10c | |
| B | Under Cover *** | 10b | |
| C | Covert Action | 10b | not recommended |
| D | Cover-up ** | 10d | |
| E | Deep Cover ** | 10b | |

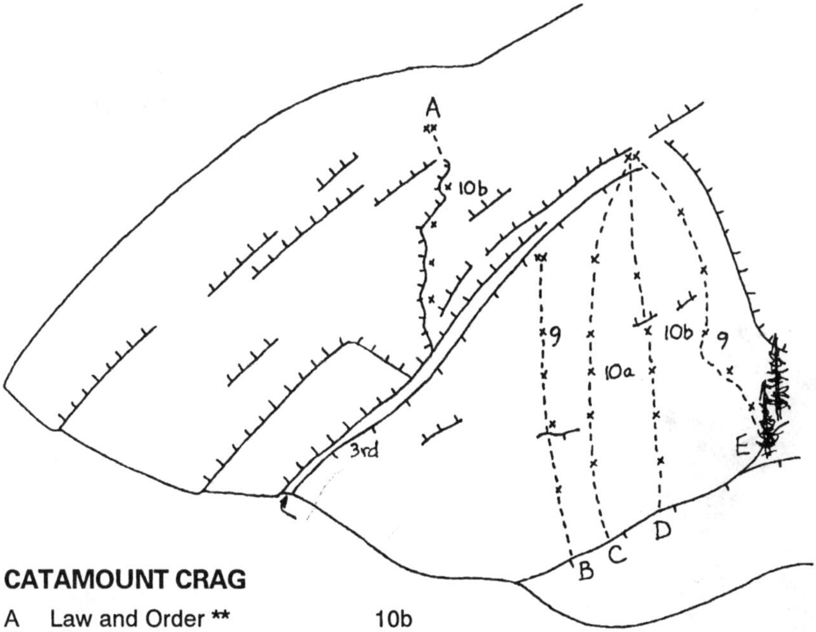

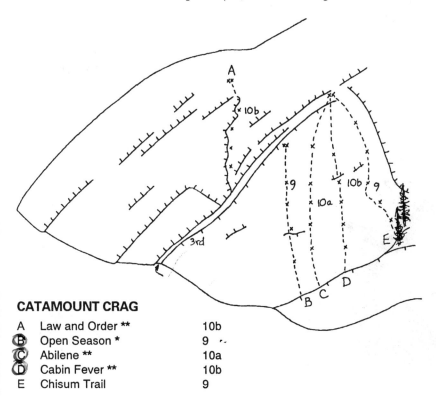

## CATAMOUNT CRAG

| | | |
|---|---|---|
| A | Law and Order ** | 10b |
| B | Open Season * | 9 |
| C | Abilene ** | 10a |
| D | Cabin Fever ** | 10b |
| E | Chisum Trail | 9 |

## HEATWAVE CLIFF

| | | |
|---|---|---|
| A | Heatwave | 10c |

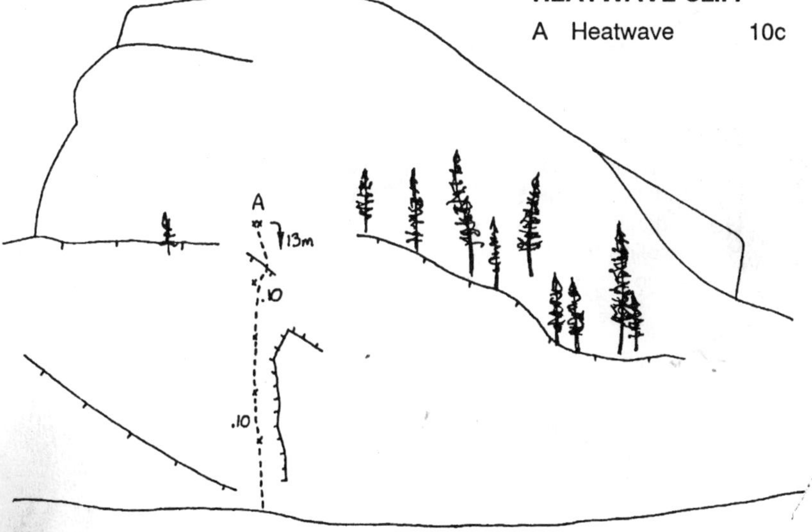

## COSMOLOGY CRAG

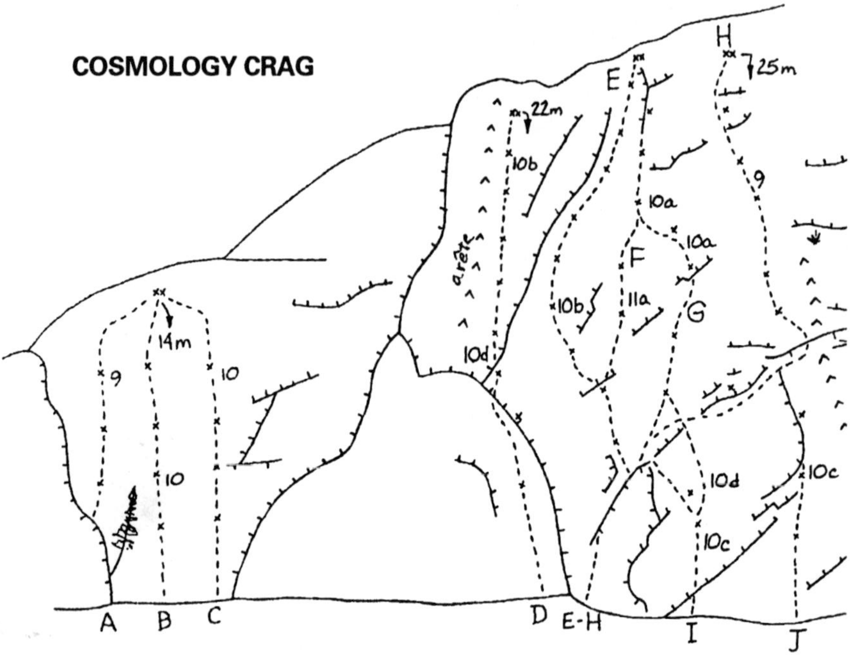


| | | |
|---|---|---|
| A | Navigator | 9 |
| B | Nine to Five ** | 10b |
| C | Cat and Mouse ** | 10c |
| D | Archaos ** | 10d |
| E | Big Bang Theory ** | 10b |
| F | Redshift Connection ** | 11a |
| G | Redshift * | 10a |
| H | Timeline ** | 9 |
| I | Indigo | 10d |

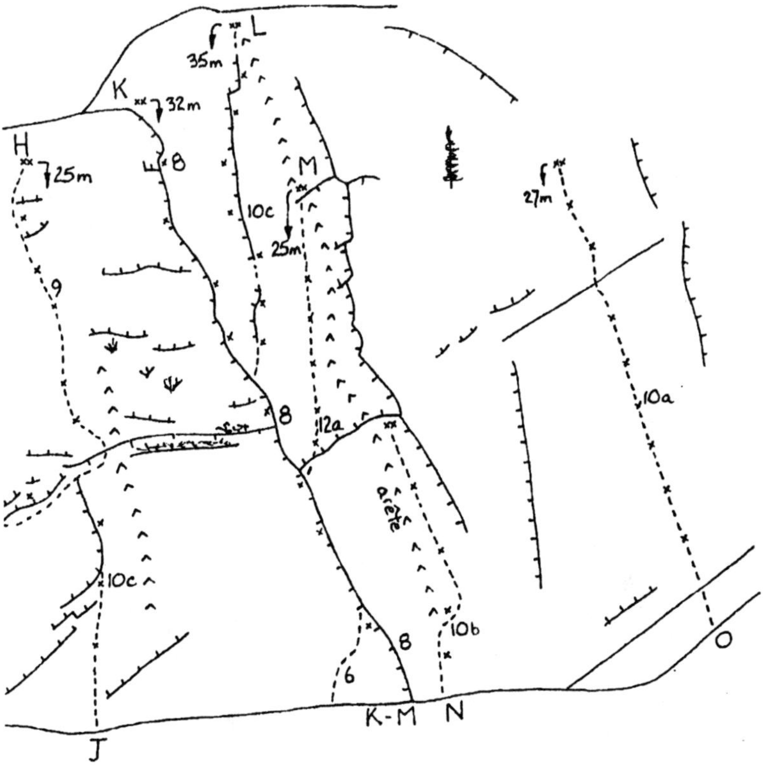


| | | |
|---|---|---|
| J | History of Time** | 10c |
| K | Cosmic String ** | 8 |
| L | Prime Cut **** | 10c |
| M | Outer Limits *** | 12a |
| N | Dead Heat | 10b |
| O | Entropy * | 10a |

*Jon Jones on Shockwave (10d), photo John Martin*

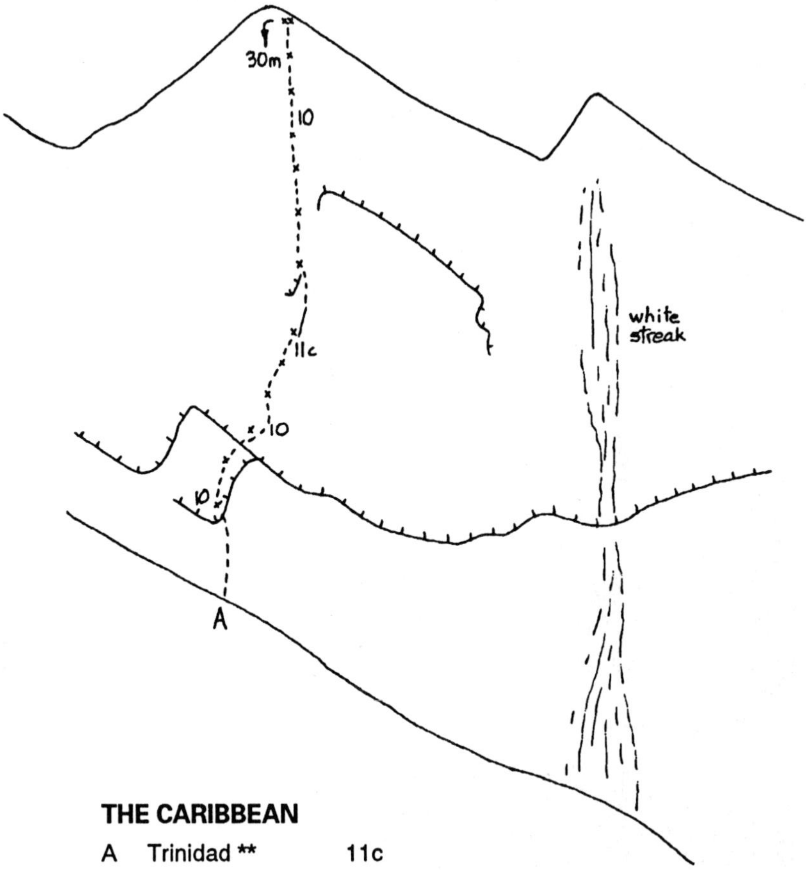


**THE CARIBBEAN**

A Trinidad ** 11c

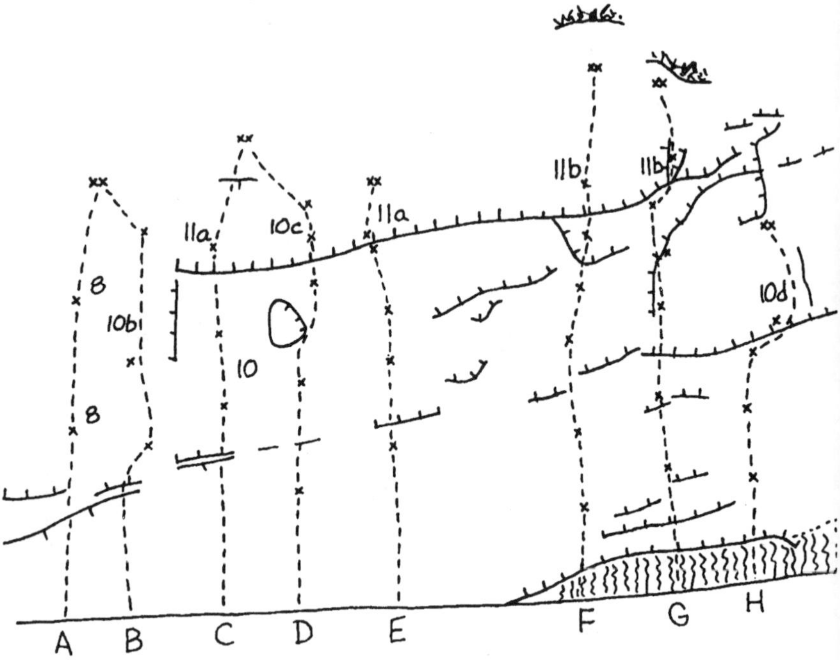


**CREEKSIDE CRAG**

| | | |
|---|---|---|
| A | Hockey Night in Canada * | 8 |
| B | Strandline ** | 10b |
| C | Dynosoar ** | 11a/b |
| D | Stone Cold ** | 10c |
| E | Some Like It Hot ** | 11a |
| F | Tilt ** | 11b |
| G | Withering Heights *** | 11b |
| H | Arcana *** | 10d |

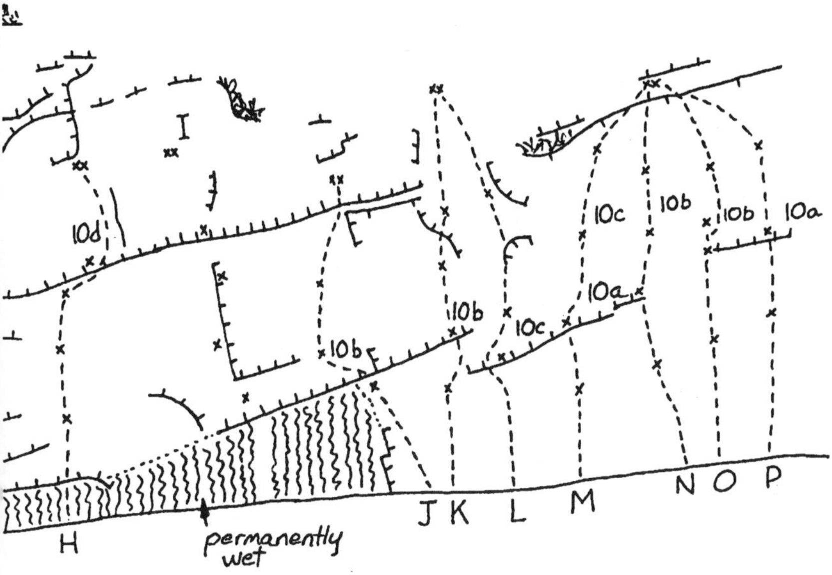


| | | |
|---|---|---|
| I | project | |
| J | Lunch Rambo Style ** | 10b |
| K | Cafe Rambo * | 10b |
| L | Lysdexia *** | 10c |
| M | When Worlds Collide ** | 10c |
| N | Gondwanaland ** | 10b |
| O | Continental Drift ** | 10b |
| P | Burmese ** | 9/10a |

## CAVERN CRAG

| | | |
|---|---|---|
| A | Natural Selection *** | 11c |
| B | Evolution ** | 10b |

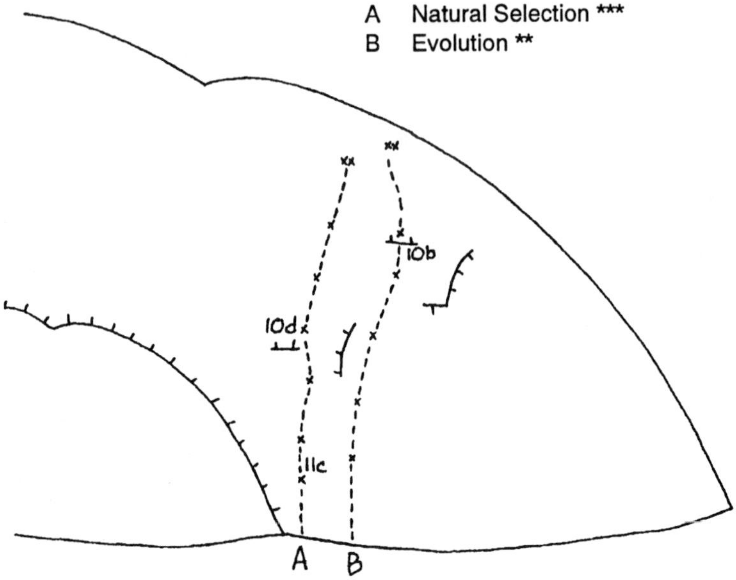


## CANADIAN FORKS

| | | |
|---|---|---|
| A | Danse Macabre ** | 11c |
| B | unknown ** | 11a |
| C | project | |
| D | Phlogiston *** | 11c |
| E | Free Lunch *** | 10c |

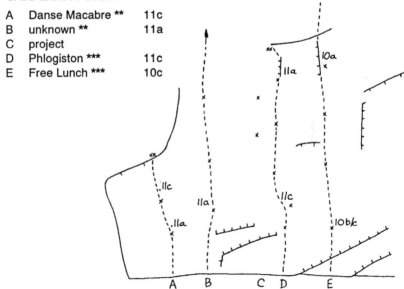

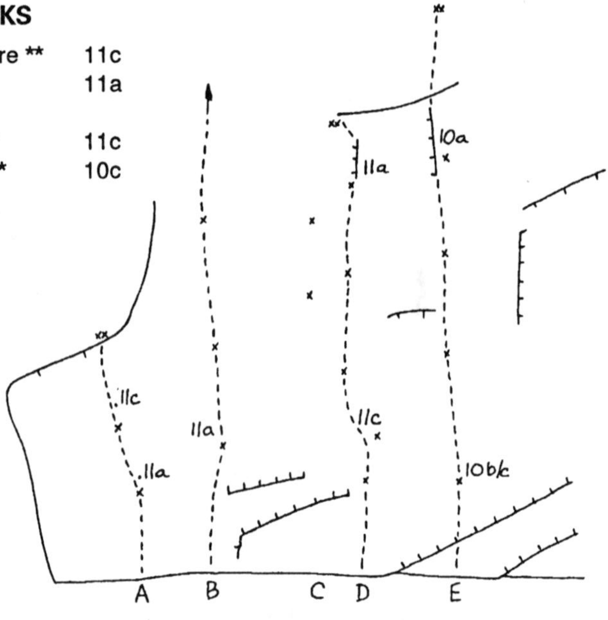

# BATAAN

Bataan is a new area high on the south side of Grotto Mountain, between the two large "grottos". It is readily visible from the valley bottom — look for a long, east-facing cliff that starts near a cave, up and left from the left end of the big quarrying/mining scar. Near timberline the cliff bends around to the right and becomes south-facing: this is Bataan. The rock here is sound, pocketed in places, and very steep. The routes completed or in progress at the time of writing were all on the south-facing portion of the cliff.

### Approach

Park at a small pull-off on the north side of Highway 1A, 1.4 km east of Indian Flats Road (the access to the Alpine Club of Canada Clubhouse). At the top of the steep slopes immediately above the parking area, cross a fence and follow flagging through mostly open forest. Shortly after passing the left end of the mining scar, follow a trail through scree and then past a prominent cave in the cliff to the left. This is the cave that can be seen from the highway. Above, the route more or less follows the base of the cliffs up to the climbing area. In terms of approach time, Bataan lives up to its name (as in The March to Bataan): expect to spend the better part of two hours getting there. Take lots of water.

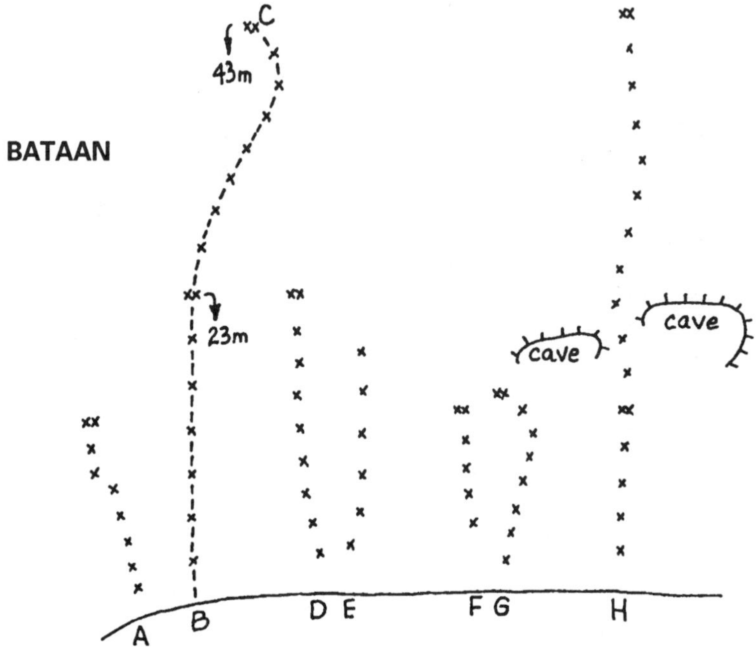


| | | | | | |
|---|---|---|---|---|---|
| A | project | | C | Truckasaurus | 12a |
| B | Nirvana | 13a | D-H | projects | |

Andy Genereux on Bandits at 2 O'clock (11b), photo Jon Jones

# CRAG X

Crag X is renowned for the appalling quality of its rock. However, recent excavations in the vicinity of Sideline have uncovered some climbs of surprisingly high quality. The southerly aspect and short approach make it possible to climb here even in winter (on warm days). The slopes around Crag X are heavily used by bighorn sheep and are consequently infested with wood ticks in spring.

**Approach**

Park at an old industrial site on the north side of Highway 1A, 1.8 km west of the Baymag #2 Plant turnoff. Follow a dirt road east around a couple of bends to a clearing under a power line. Follow a prominent trail to the north through the trees for a couple of minutes until another trail heads up a steep slope on the left to the base of Crag X (10 minutes from the highway). *Sideline* is the prominent corner above a very large tree about 40m east (right) of the top of the trail.

**CRAG X**

| | | | |
|---|---|---|---|
| A | X-terminator *** | 10c | |
| B | Sideline *** | 9 | gear to 2" |
| B' | Sideline Variations | | |
| C | Double Cross ** | 10c | |
| C' | Double Cross Direct * | 12a | |
| D | Mainline * | 10c | |
| E | Mr. Clean | 11b/c | |
| F | Saigon Kiss *** | 11d | |
| G | Bombs Away ** | 11c | nuts, Friend 2.5, small TCU |
| H | Bandits at 2 O'clock **** | 11b | |
| I | Pilot Error * | 10c | Friends to 3, med nuts |
| J | Both Guns Blazing ** | 11d | RP3, nuts |
| K | Bomb Bay Groove | | |

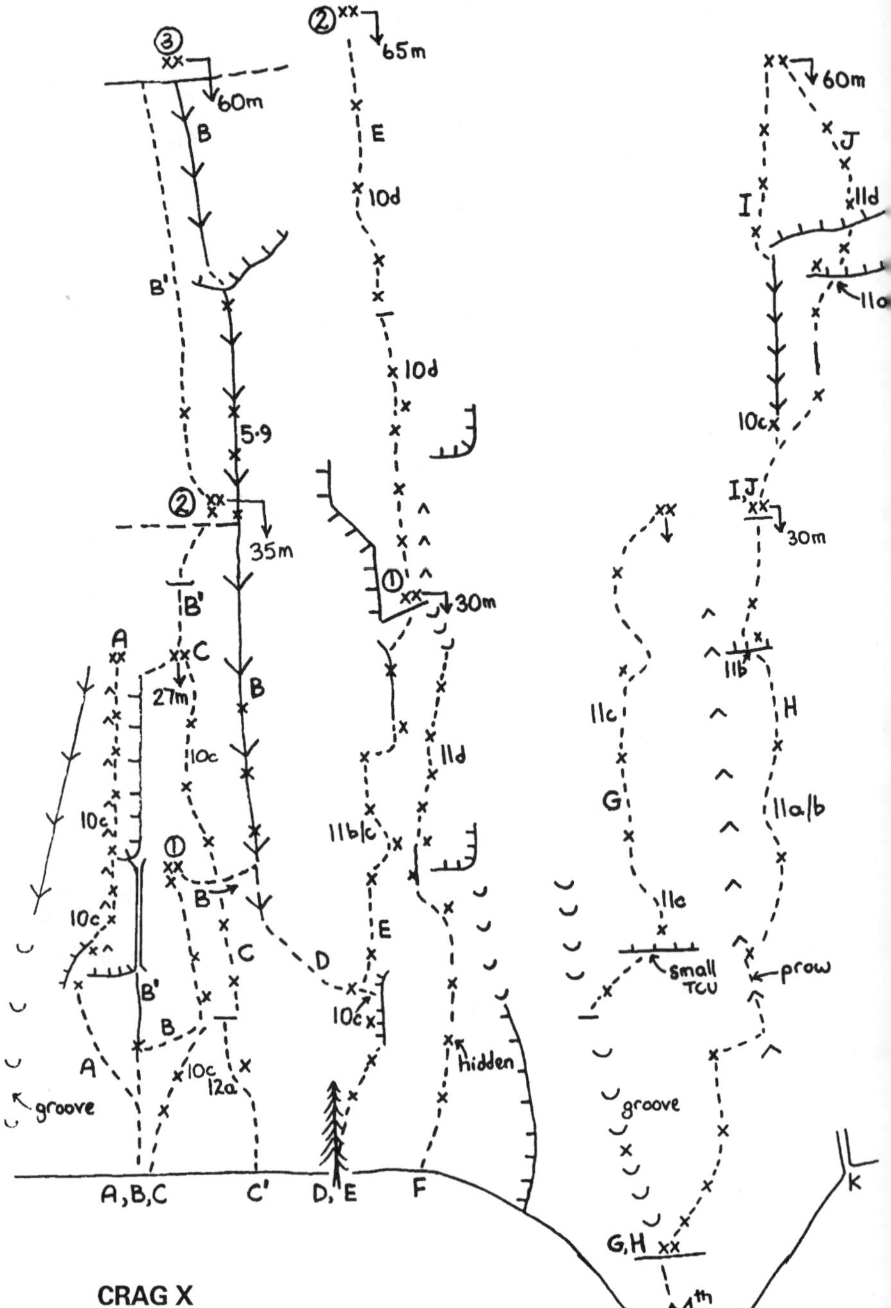
65m
60m
60m
E
10d
10d
B
B'
5.9
35m
30m
30m
27m
10c
11d
11b/c
10c
10c
11c
11a/b
11b
11c
G
H
I
J
I,J
11d
11a
10c
small TCU
prow
hidden
groove
groove
12a
A
B
C
D
A,B,C
C'
D, E
F
G,H
K
4th

CRAG X

# GROTTO CANYON

Grotto Canyon is located in the deep valley immediately east of Grotto Mountain. Many of the climbs are modern sport routes but some were established from the ground up and others date from the early days of rap bolting, when protection was often sketchy by today's standards. Consequently, some of the climbs require gear, some have loose rock, some are poorly protected (especially near the ground), and some lack proper top anchors. A few of these earlier routes have recently been retrofitted and others are likely to be in the near future. Route polishing has occurred on several cliffs, Illusion Rock being the most badly affected. The routes here have become slippery, unpleasant and dangerous to lead as a result of excessive toproping. Sunshine is often hard to find in Grotto Canyon, and several of the cliffs languish in perpetual shade. In the main canyon, Hemingway Wall is the only climbing area that catches morning sun; Water Wall Right, Paintings Wall South, the Upper Right Wing and the Upper Narrows are the sunniest places in the afternoon. The Alley catches late afternoon and evening sun. Farther upstream, Hoodoo Crag is warm in the morning and the Upper Tier in the afternoon. A few of the climbs in The Narrows require two ropes; one is enough everywhere else.

Several of the climbs on Water Wall Right have been manufactured by drilling holes in the rock, gluing on new holds, and so on. As well, Tropicana (on Hemingway Wall) has enhanced holds. As indicated in the introduction to this guide, the majority local concensus is that these are inappropriate methods of establishing new climbs, and the manufactured climbs are included in this guide only for the sake of completeness.

**Approach**

The recommended approach starts from a gravel parking lot north of Highway 1A, 4.5 km west of the Heart Mountain Cafe in Exshaw. If you are coming from the west, look for the parking lot partway around the first bend to the left past Gap Lake and Crag X. A narrow trail starts just a few metres left (west) of the parking lot entrance. After skirting the west side of the Baymag #2 Plant, the trail leads to a powerline right of way at some large boulders after about 5 minutes. Continue north over a grassy knoll (the Baymag water supply reservoir) 2 minutes to the canyon mouth. From this point the main "trail" follows the stream bed, crossing the creek numerous times. The first four creek crossings can be avoided by a trail through the trees on the right (east) bank. It is possible to shorten the walk by driving along the power line right of way, starting from the Baymag access road; however, large rocks, a mudhole, and potential conflicts with hikers make this option hardly worth the effort. In fact it is technically illegal to drive the power line access road because it is a designated hiking trail.

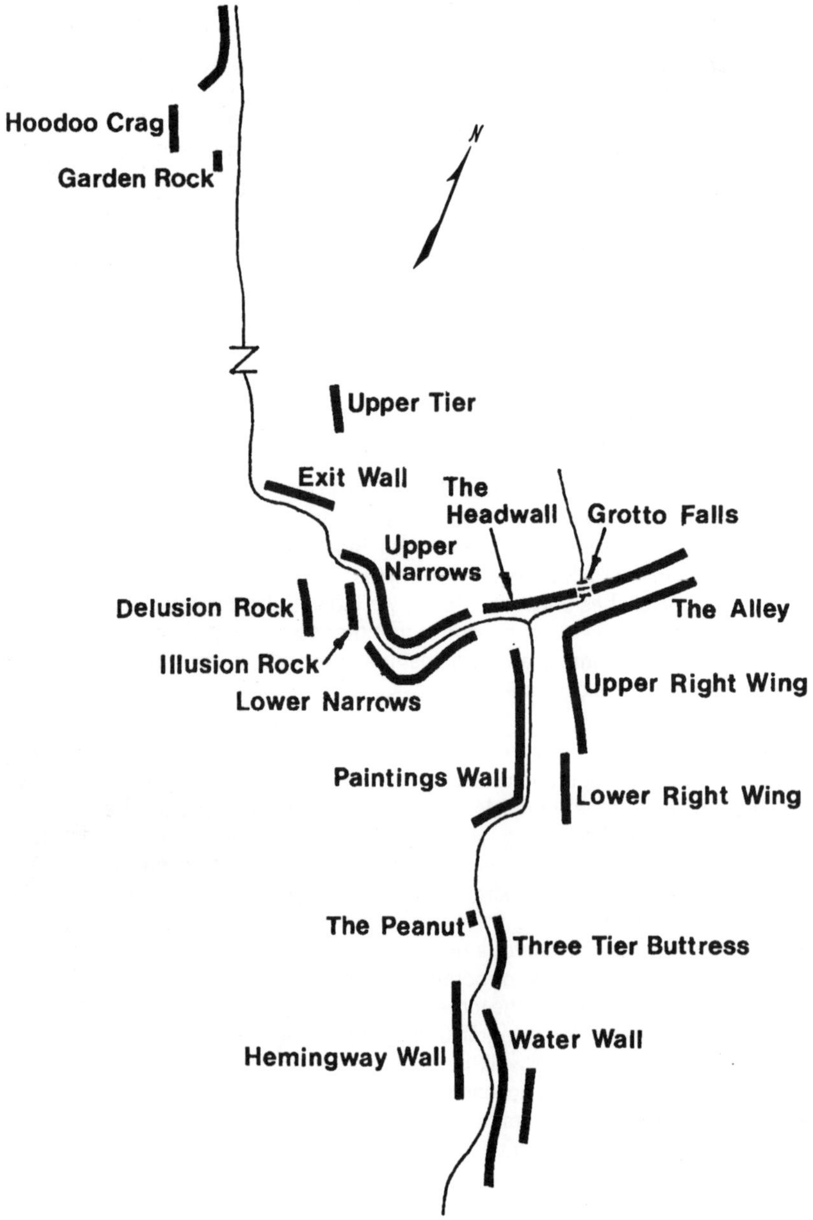
Hoodoo Crag
Garden Rock
N
Upper Tier
Exit Wall
The Headwall
Grotto Falls
Upper Narrows
Delusion Rock
The Alley
Illusion Rock
Lower Narrows
Upper Right Wing
Paintings Wall
Lower Right Wing
The Peanut
Three Tier Buttress
Water Wall
Hemingway Wall

*Simon Parboosingh on Metabolica (13a), photo Andy Genereux*

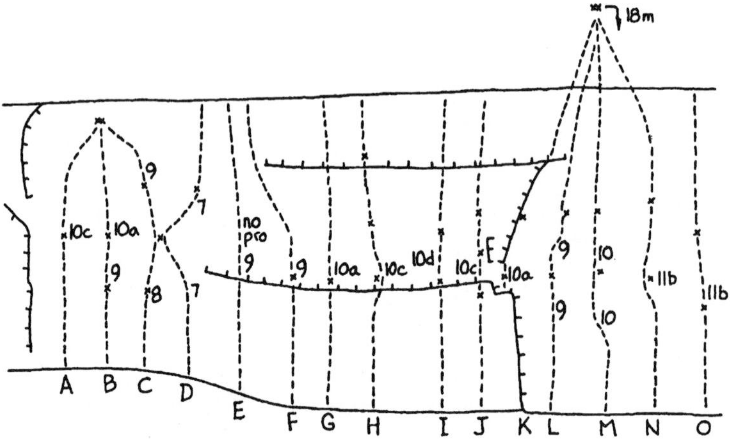


## WATER WALL, LEFT

| | | |
|---|---|---|
| A | Raindust | 10c |
| B | Soft Option ** | 10a/b |
| C | Kinesthesia ** | 9 |
| D | Breezin' * | 7 |
| E | Ill Wind | 9 |
| F | Canary in a Coal Mine | 9 |
| G | Deviant Behaviour | 10a |
| H | Loose Lips Sink Ships | 10c |
| I | Lip Service * | 10d |
| J | Power Play ** | 10c |
| K | Spring Clean * | 10a |
| L | Last Call * | 9/10a |
| M | The Ablutor ** | 10c |
| N | Scarface keep walking | 11b |
| O | For Whom the Bell Tolls * | 11b |

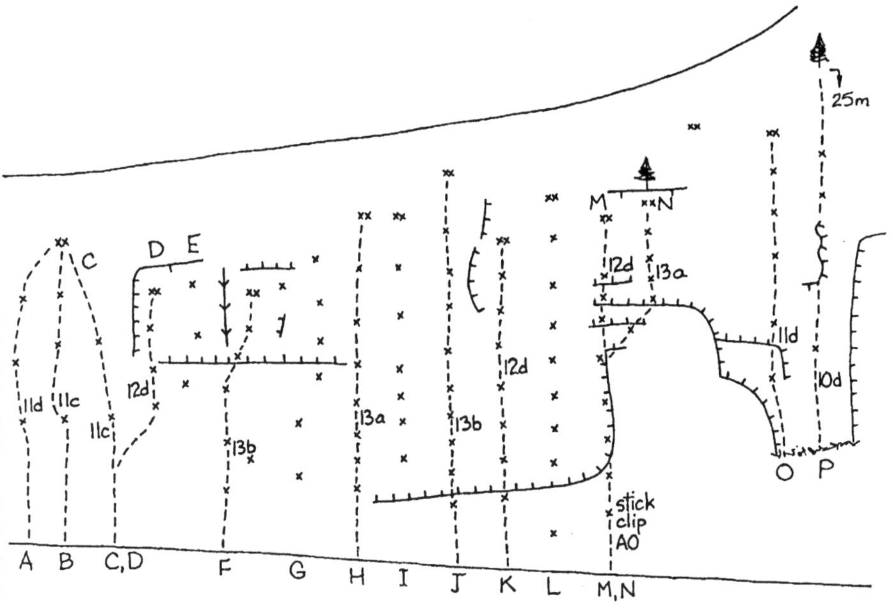


## WATER WALL, RIGHT

| | | | |
|---|---|---|---|
| A | Reflex Action | 11d | |
| B | Cerebral Goretex | 11c | |
| C | Across the River and into the Trees | 11c | |
| D | Cause and Effect | 12c/d | manufactured |
| E | project | | |
| F | Burn Hollywood Burn | 13b | manufactured |
| G | project | | |
| H | Shep's Diner | 13a | manufactured |
| I | project | | |
| J | The Resurrection | 13b | manufactured |
| K | Crimes of Passion | 12c/d | manufactured |
| L | project | | |
| M | Tintin and Snowy Get Psyched **** | 12d | |
| N | Metabolica *** | 13a | |
| O | Urban Youth | 11d | |
| P | The Sting * | 10d | |

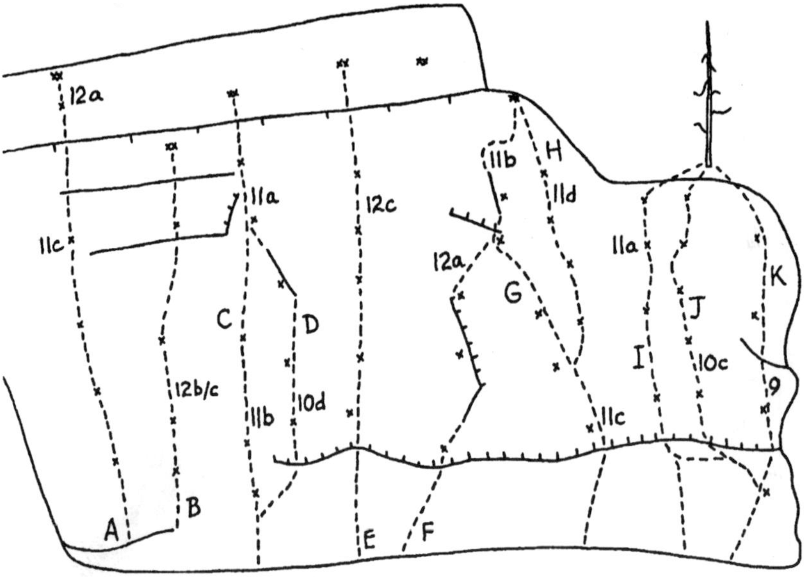


## HEMINGWAY WALL, LEFT

| | | | |
|---|---|---|---|
| A | The Importance of Being Ernest **** | 12a | |
| B | Cracked Rhythm ** | 12b/c | |
| C | Chips Are for Kids *** | 11b | |
| D | Farewell to Arms ***** | 11a | |
| E | Tropicana | 12c | chipped holds |
| F | Success Pool **** | 12a | |
| G | Walk on the Wilde Side ***** | 11c | |
| H | Stone Age Romeos **** | 11d | |
| I | Grey Matter ** | 11a | |
| J | Grand Larceny *** | 10c/d | |
| K | Falling from Heaven *** | 9 | Second, Lead, LEAD |

## HEMINGWAY WALL, RIGHT

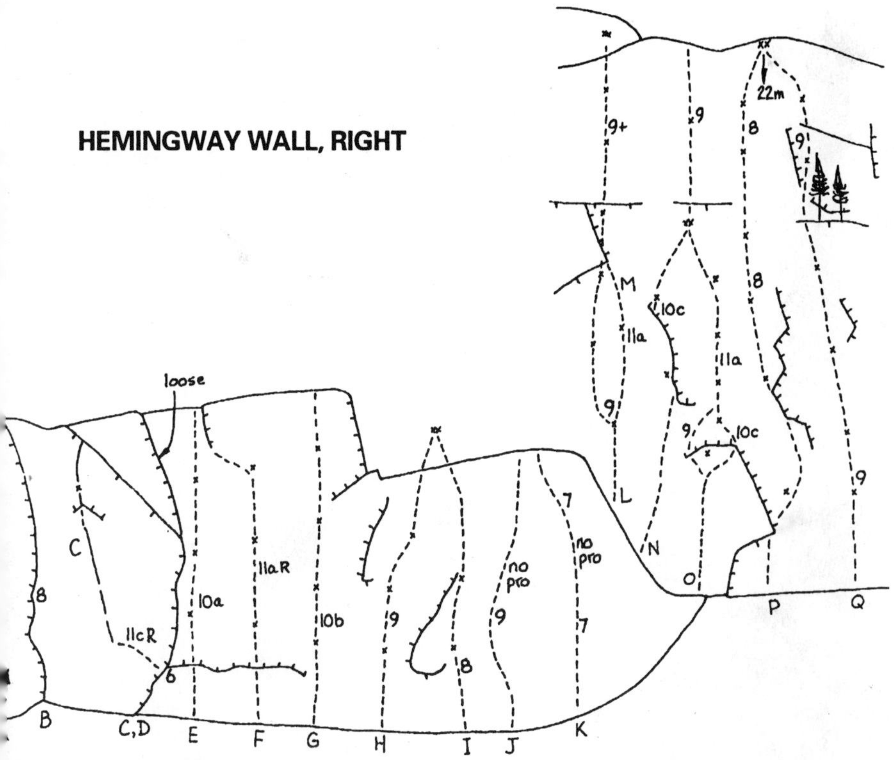


| | | | |
|---|---|---|---|
| A | Falling from Heaven *** | 9 | |
| B | Little Canadian Corner * | 8 | gear to 3" |
| C | Lively Up Yourself | 11c | gear to 2" |
| D | Flake Line | 6 | not recommended |
| E | Runaway | 10a | |
| F | Footloose | 11a | not recommended |
| G | Run of the River *** | 10b | |
| H | Walk the Line * | 9 | |
| I | Cakewalk * | 8 | |
| J | Oh No Not Another | 9 | |
| K | Yet Another | 7 | |
| L | Layla ** | 9/10a | |
| M | Delilah ** | 11a | |
| N | Temptress *** | 10c | |
| O | Siren Song *** | 11a | |
| P | Nymphet ** | 8 Lead, Lead | |
| Q | Scheherazade ** | 9 | |

*Lynda Howard on Falling from Heaven (9), photo John Martin*

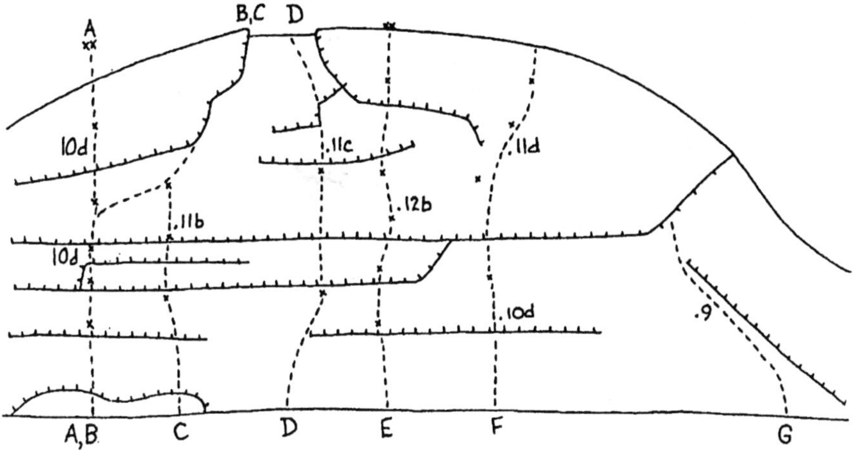


## THREE TIER BUTTRESS

| | | |
|---|---|---|
| A | Stiff Upper Lip * | 10d |
| B | Short and Curly * | 10d |
| C | Too Low for Zero * | 11b |
| D | High Octane ** | 11c |
| E | Dr. No ** | 12b |
| F | Mr. Olympia ** | 11d |
| G | Rising Damp | 9 |

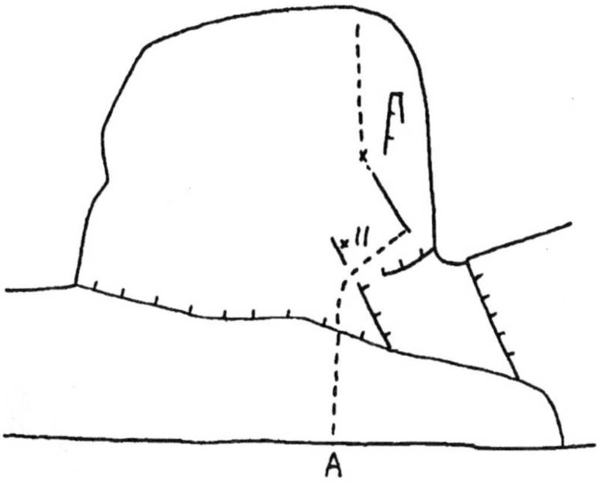


## THE PEANUT

| | | |
|---|---|---|
| A | K.P. Special | 11a |

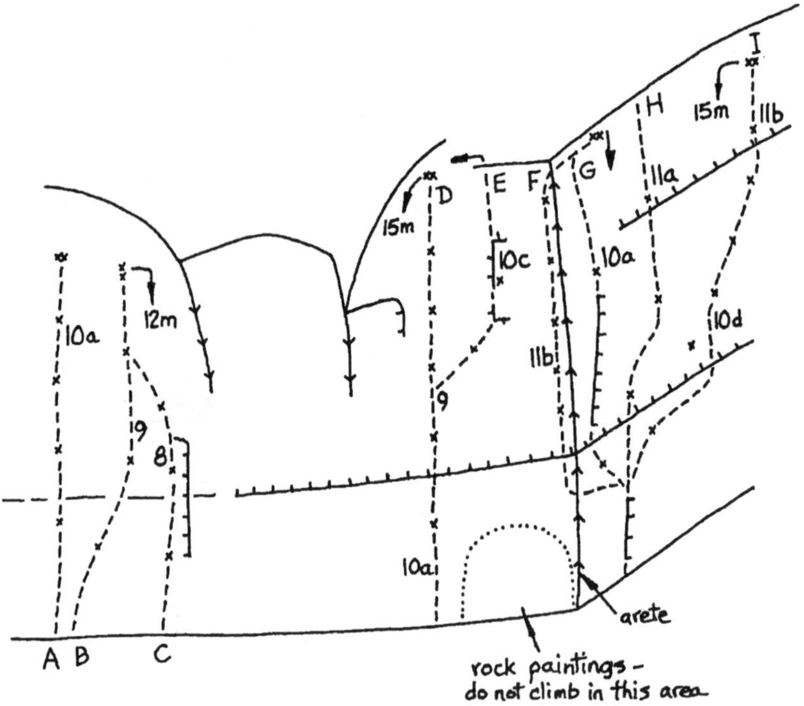


## PAINTINGS WALL, SOUTH

| | | | |
|---|---|---|---|
| A | Blaster * | 10a | |
| B | Scavenger** | 9 | |
| C | OK Corral ** | 8 | |
| D | Art of the Ancients *** | 10a | |
| E | Left to Chance | 10c | |
| F | Cultural Imperative *** | 11b | |
| G | Artful Dodger * | 10a | gear to 1.5" |
| H | Peter Pan | 11a | |
| I | Sidewinder *** | 11b | |

*John Martin on Cultural Imperative (11b), photo Andy Genereux*

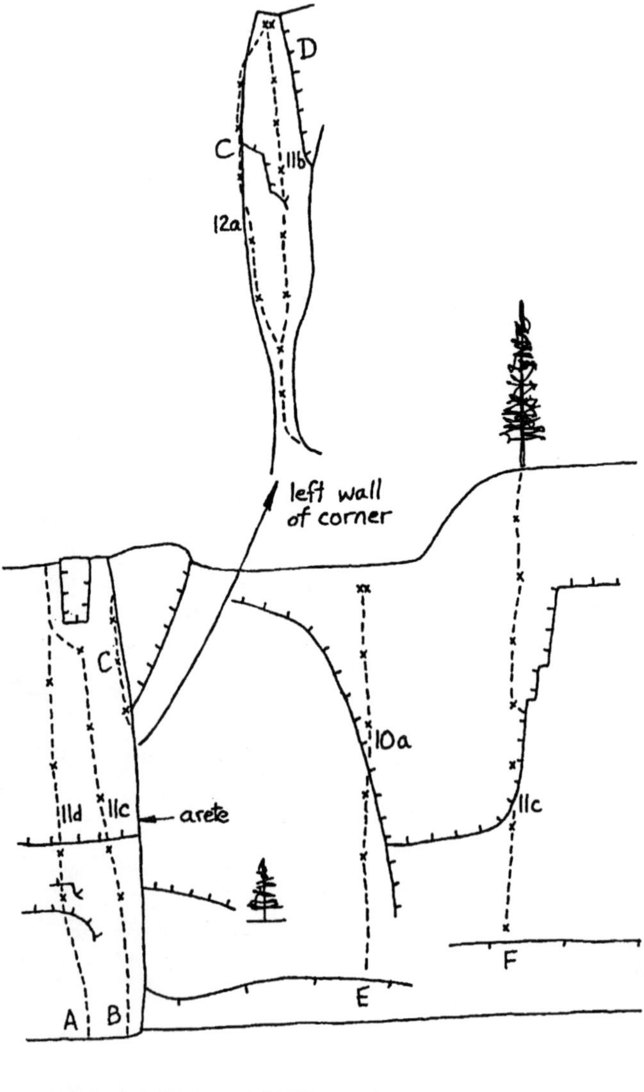


## PAINTINGS WALL, NORTH

| | | |
|---|---|---|
| A | Hellen Damnation * | 11d |
| B | Tower of Pisa ** | 11c |
| C | Tour de Force **** | 12a |
| D | Tour de Pump * | 11b |
| E | Jugthuggery *** | 10a/b |
| F | Fly By Night ** | 11c |

| | | |
|---|---|---|
| G | project | |
| H | Fast Forward * | 10c |
| I | Walk Don't Run ** | 11b |
| J | Rush ** | 11b |
| K | project | |
| L | Layaway Plan ** | 10c |
| M | Watusi Wedding **** | 10a |
| N | Jesus Drives a Cadillac ** | 10b |

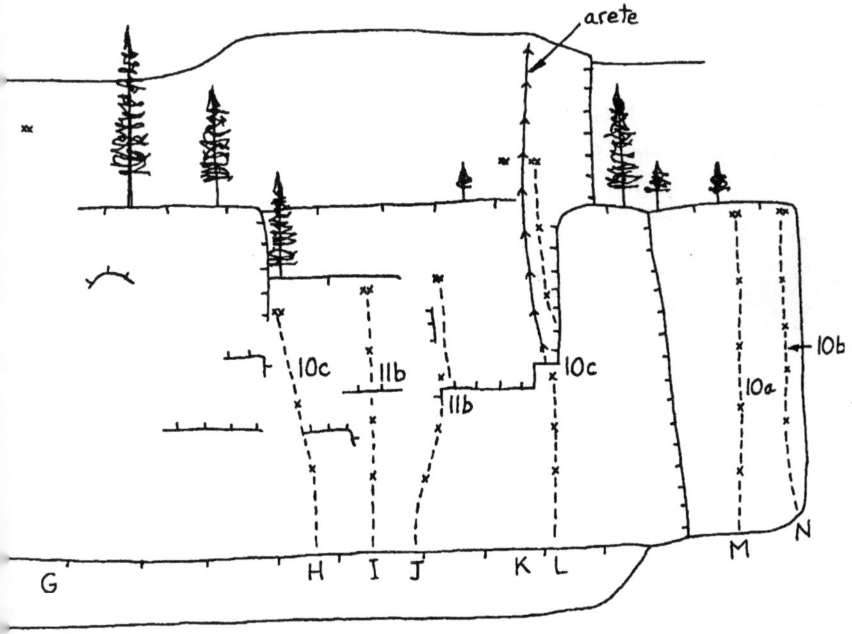

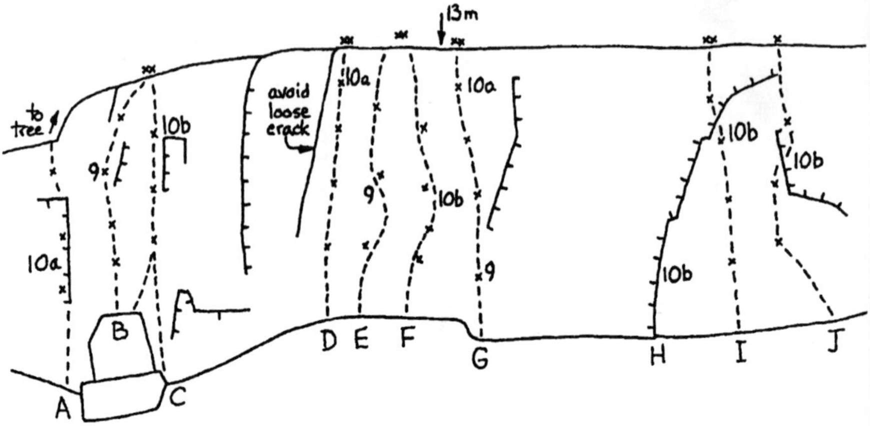


## UPPER RIGHT WING

| | | | |
|---|---|---|---|
| A | Knight Shift | 10a | |
| B | Cameo ** | 9 | |
| C | Diamond Sky | 10b | |
| D | Tapdance * | 10a | |
| E | Yellow Wedge ** | 9 | |
| F | Lemon Pie ** | 10b | |
| G | Pink Cadillac *** | 10a | Lead |
| H | Pitrun ** | 10b | gear to 2.5" |
| I | Caught in the Crossfire *** | 10b | |
| J | Supplication * | 10b | |

The **Lower Right Wing** is most conveniently reached by heading up and left along a trail that starts across the creek from Art of the Ancients (Paintings Wall). Continue up and left to get to the **Upper Right Wing.** The Upper Right Wing is also readily accessible from the fork in the creek at the base of The Headwall.

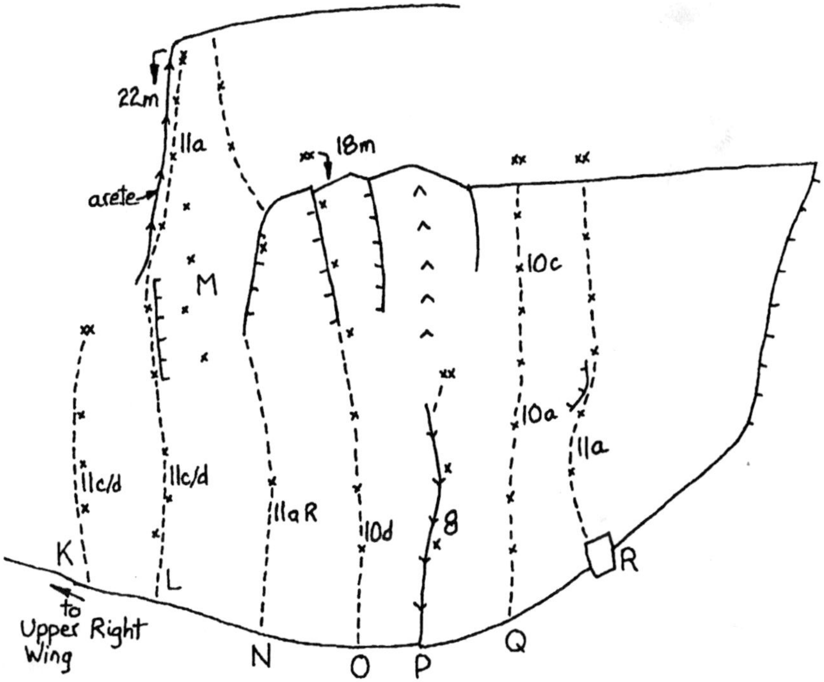


## LOWER RIGHT WING

| | | | |
|---|---|---|---|
| A | project | | |
| B | Hush ** | 11c/d | |
| C | Subliminal Seduction ** | 11c/d | |
| D | project | | |
| E | Lunatic Madness | 11a(R) | not recommended |
| F | Lithium ** | 10d | |
| G | Joyride * | 8 | |
| H | Aggressive Treatment ** | 10c/d | |
| I | Night Life ** | 11a | |

**The Alley** is reached by turning right at the base of The Headwall and scrambling up a steep trail on the right side of the creek. Head up and away from the creek at the first obvious opportunity.

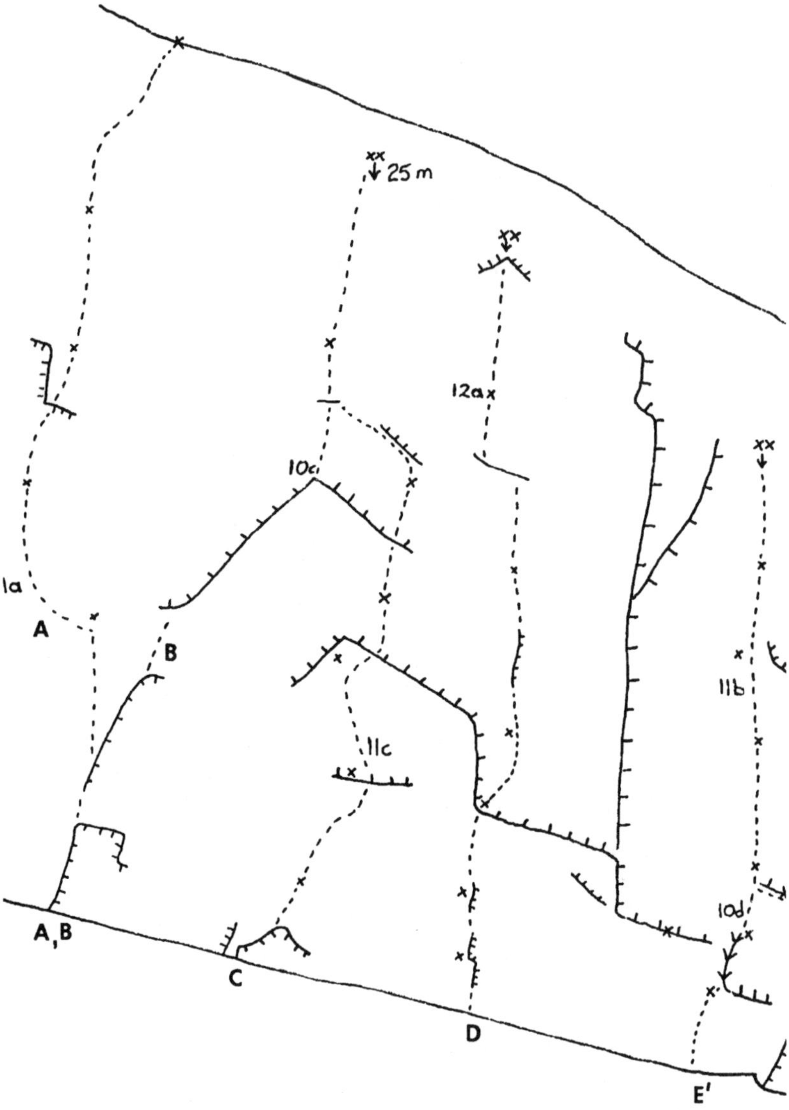

## THE ALLEY

| | | |
|---|---|---|
| A | Knight Moves * | 11a |
| B | Hollow Victory | 10c |
| C | Barchetta **** | 11c |
| D | Path of the Moose * | 12a |
| E | Submission **** | 11d |
| E' | Submission Direct **** | 11b |
| F | Crossroad ** | 11d |
| G | Snakes and Ladders ** | 12a |
| H | Fear No Art *** | 11b |
| I | Big Breasted Girls Go to the Beach and Take Their Tops Off *** | 11a |
| J | Grace Under Pressure **** | 11d |
| K | Tears of the Dinosaur * | 11b |
| L | Engines Burning *** | 11b |

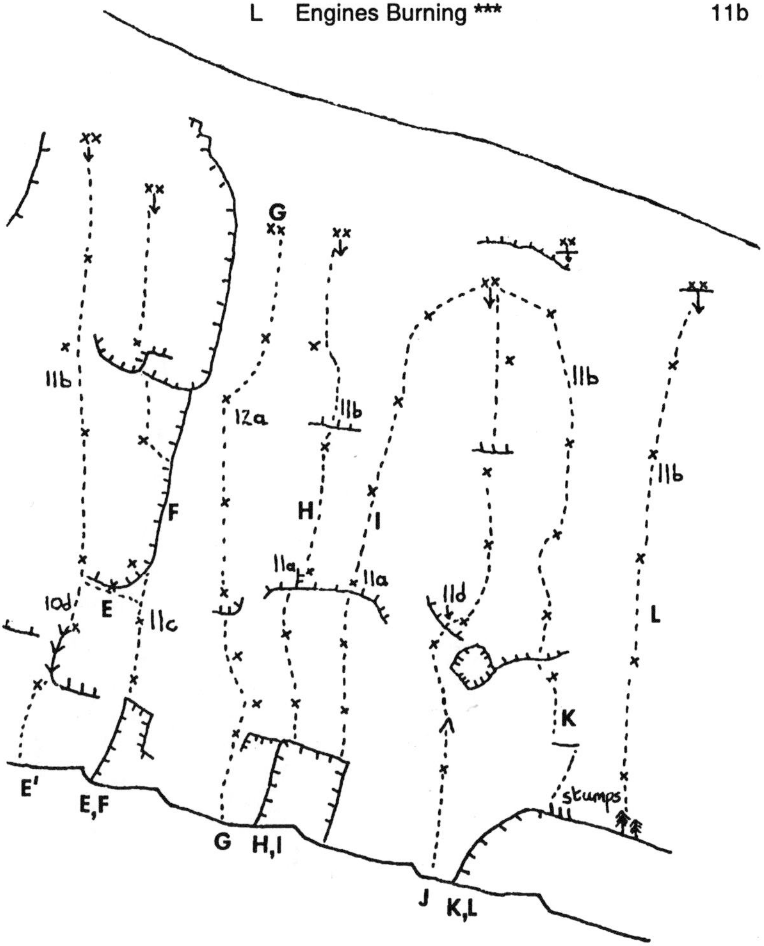

*Andy Genereux on Barchetta (11c), photo Jon Jones*

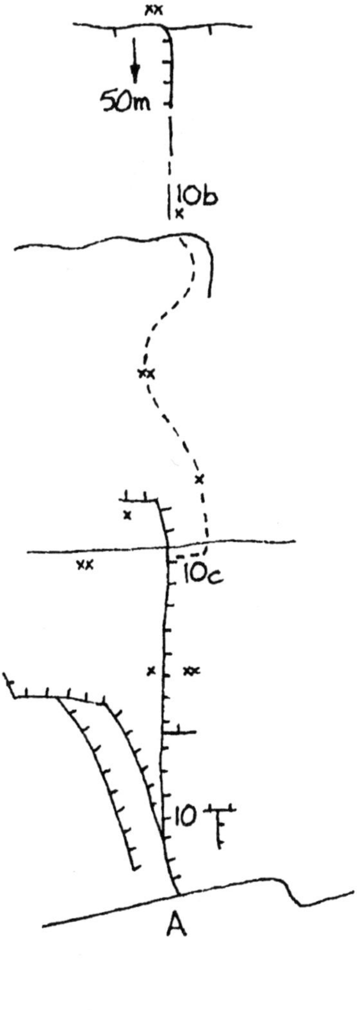


**THE HEADWALL**

| | | | |
|---|---|---|---|
| A | Verdict, The ** | 10c | gear to 3" |

## LOWER NARROWS

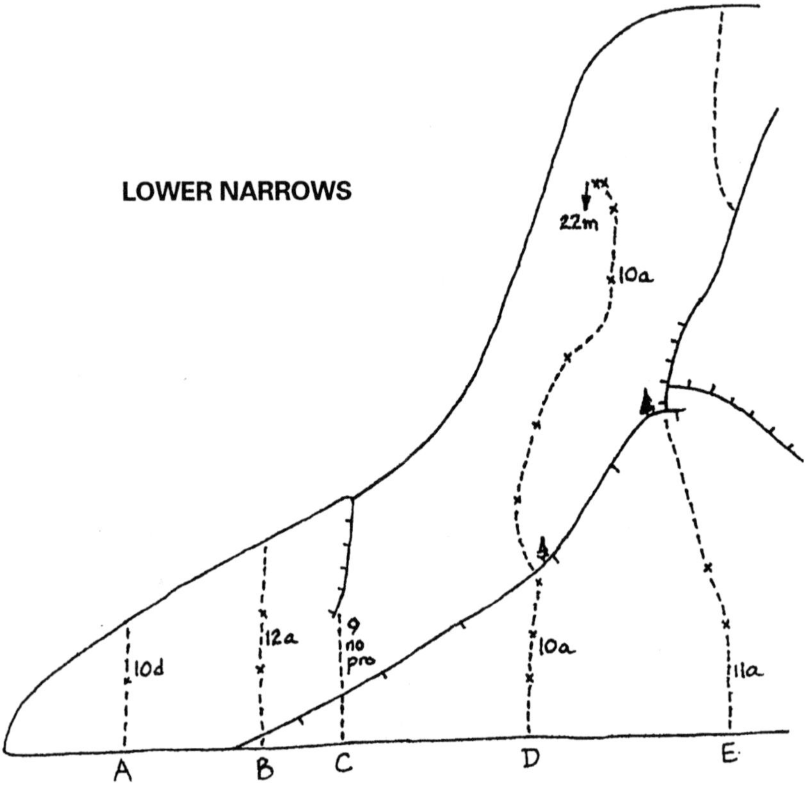


| | | | |
|---|---|---|---|
| A | Bogus | 10d | |
| B | Mighty Mite ** | 12a | |
| C | The Midden | 9 | |
| D | Xanadu *** | 10a/b | |
| E | Stormy Weather | 11a | gear to Friend 3 |

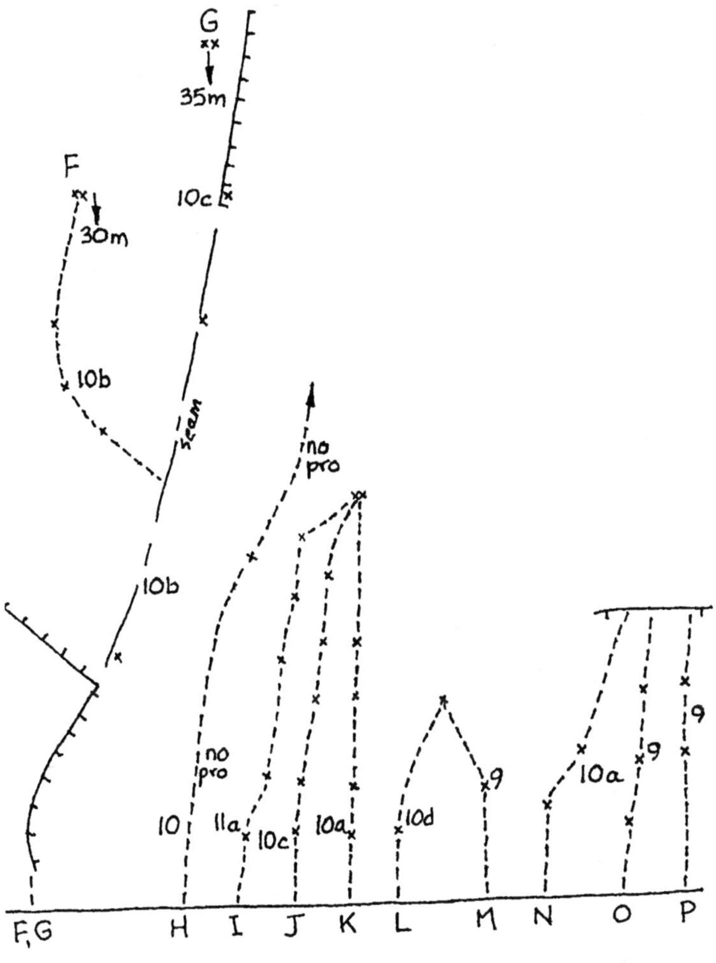


| | | | |
|---|---|---|---|
| F | Blik * | 10b | gear to Friend 3 |
| G | West Coast Idea * | 10c | gear to Friend 3 |
| H | Moonabago | 10b | not recommended |
| I | Mendocino * | 11a | |
| J | Malibu * | 10c | |
| K | Monterey * | 10a | |
| L | Baker Street | 10d | |
| M | Dr. Watson | 9 | |
| N | Lost World | 10a | |
| O | Hollow Earth * | 9 | |
| P | Moriarty | 9 | |

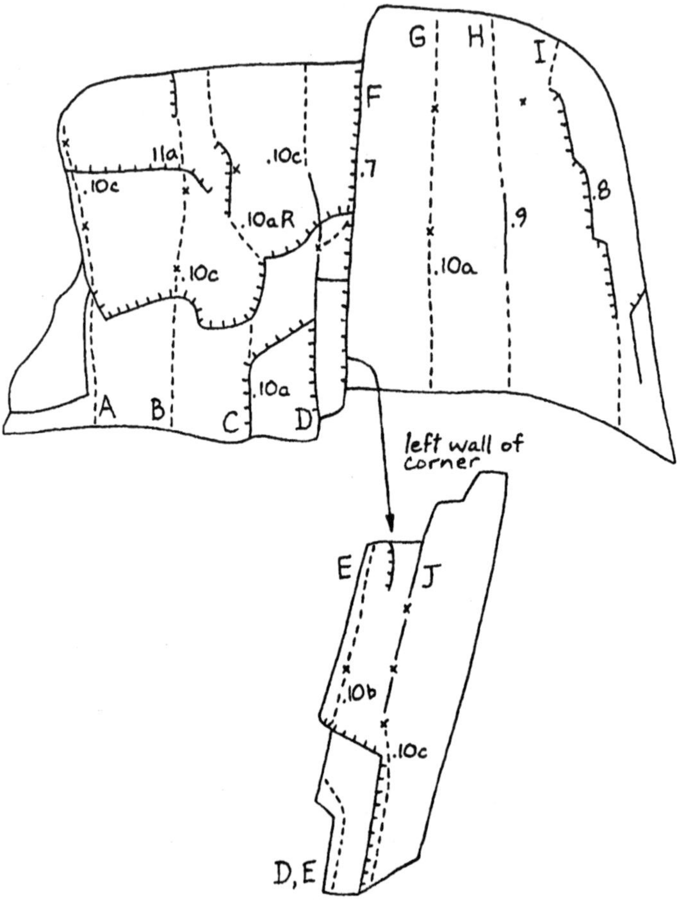


**ILLUSION ROCK**

| | | | |
|---|---|---|---|
| A | Harder Than It Looks | 10c | |
| B | Monkey in a Rage ** | 11a | |
| C | Grand Illusion ** | 10a | |
| D | The Grander Illusion *** | 10c | RP's, small Rocks |
| E | Guitarzan * | 10b | |
| F | Jackorner ** | 7 | gear to 3" |
| G | Impending Impact *** | 10a | |
| H | Tiny Tim | 9 | |
| I | Yonge Street | 8 | |
| J | George of the Jungle *** | 10c | |

**Delusion Rock** lies a couple of minutes uphill from the top of Illusion Rock.

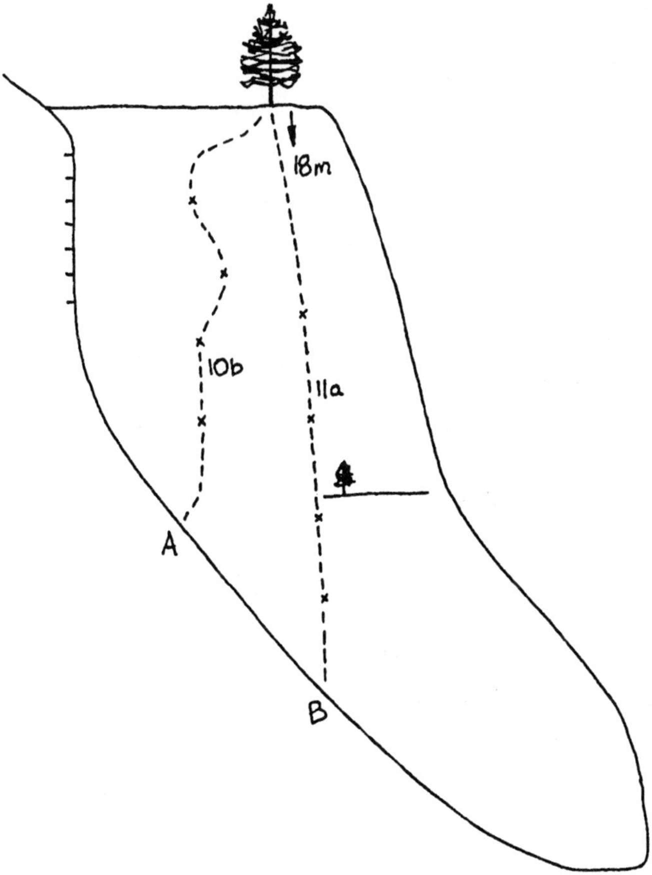


**DELUSION ROCK**

| | | |
|---|---|---|
| A | Burnt Weenie Sandwich * | 10b |
| B | Grand Delusion * | 11a |

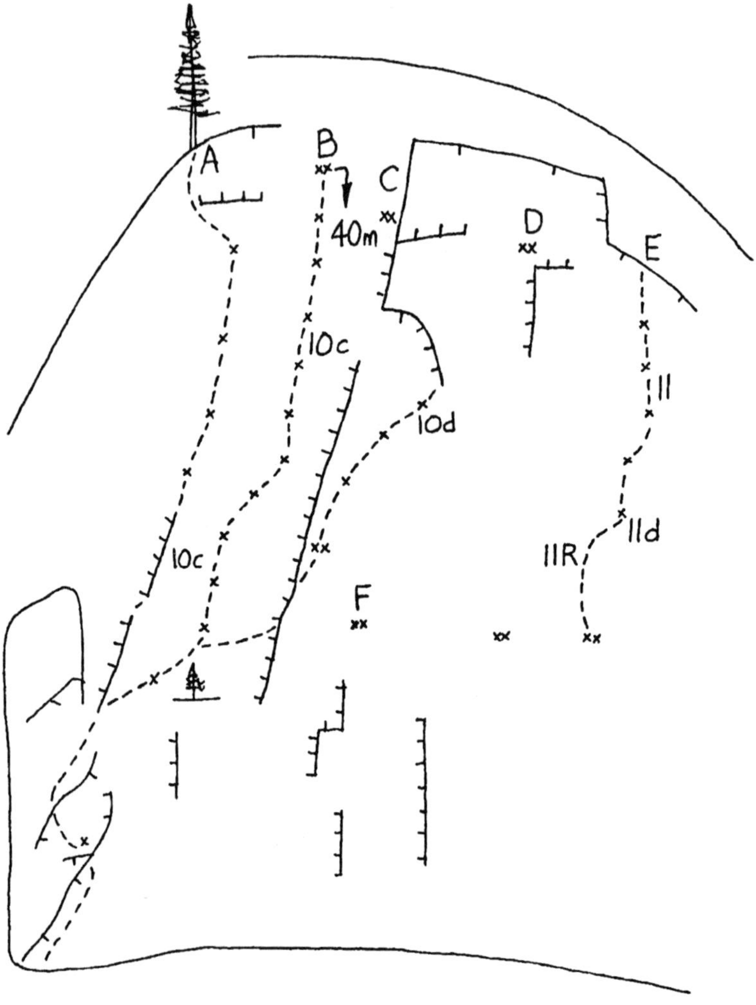


## UPPER NARROWS

| | | | |
|---|---|---|---|
| A | Trading Places ** | 10c | small wires & Friends, TCUs |
| B | Undertow ** | 10c | small wires, Friend 2 |
| C | Tabernaquered | 10d | small wires, Friends 2-3.5 |
| D | project | | |
| E | Mirage | 11d (R) | rap to start |
| F | project | | |

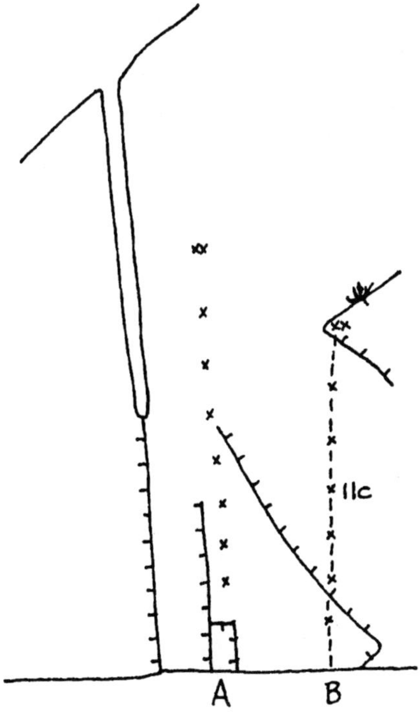


**EXIT WALL**

| | | |
|---|---|---|
| A | project | |
| B | Blackened | 11c/d |

The **Upper Tier** is a steep, prickly slab of nearly impeccable rock high up on the east side of the canyon just beyond the end of The Narrows. Walk about 150m past the upstream end of The Narrows and start up at a little scree slope near a small, yellowish outcrop of glacial till. Work up and right past small, slabby cliff bands to reach the forest below the Upper Tier, then go up and left to reach the climbs. The approach takes about 15 minutes from the valley floor. Take a small selection of nuts and Friends.

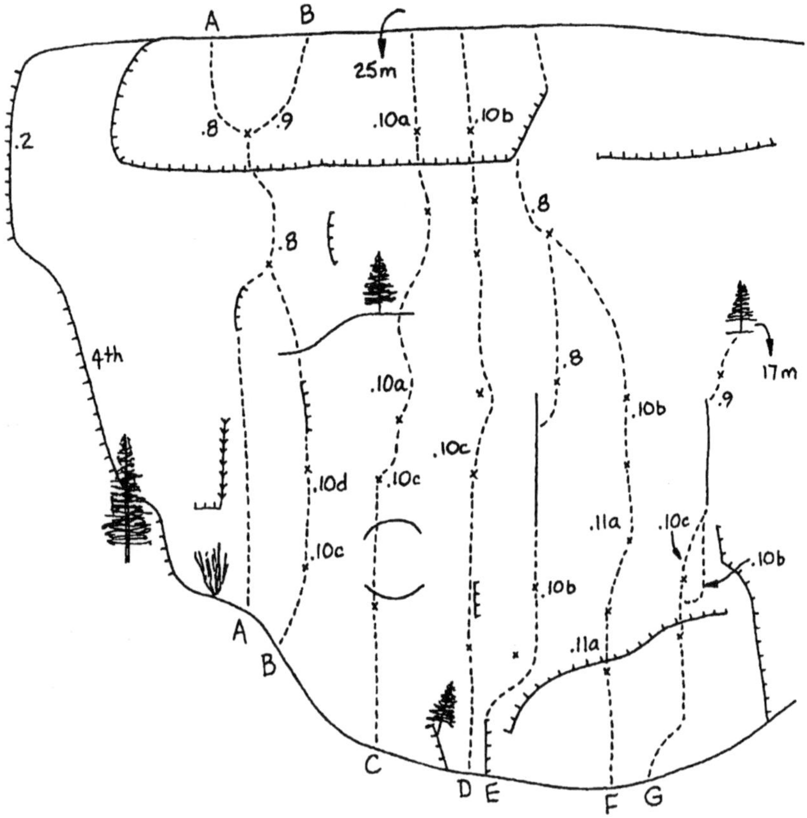


## UPPER TIER

| | | | |
|---|---|---|---|
| A | Fat City * | 8 | small wired nuts |
| B | Excitable Boy *** | 10d | |
| C | Mandala *** | 10c | RP 3 |
| D | Rat Patrol ** | 10c | |
| E | Search Pattern *** | 10b | small wires, Friends 1 & 3.5 |
| F | Facelift **** | 11a | |
| G | Squirrel Breath *** | 10b/c | wired nuts |

**Garden Rock** is a small cliff in the valley bottom just beyond a large cave in the glacial till formations on the west side of the valley.

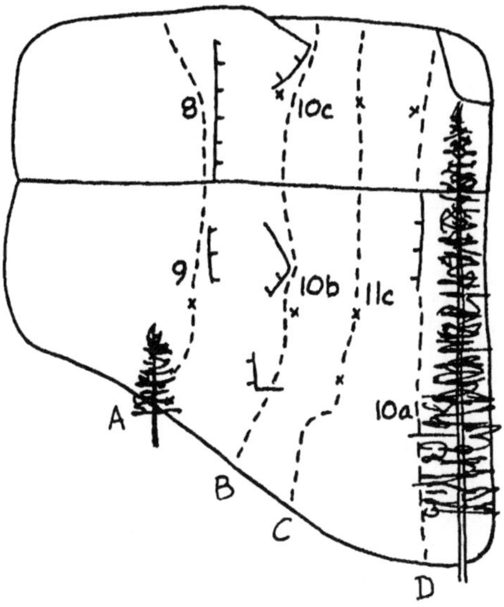


## GARDEN ROCK

| | | | |
|---|---|---|---|
| A | Pining Away ** | 9 | wired nuts |
| B | Conifer Crack *** | 10c | Friend 3 |
| C | Chainsaw Wall | 11c | |
| D | All Spruced Up ** | 10a | small wired nuts |

**Hoodoo Crag** is a little farther upstream than Garden Rock and about 75 m up from the valley floor. The easiest approach starts at the base of Armadillo Buttress, the large cliff just beyond Garden Rock. Work up and left, following the base of Armadillo Buttress at first, for about 5 minutes to get to the cliff.

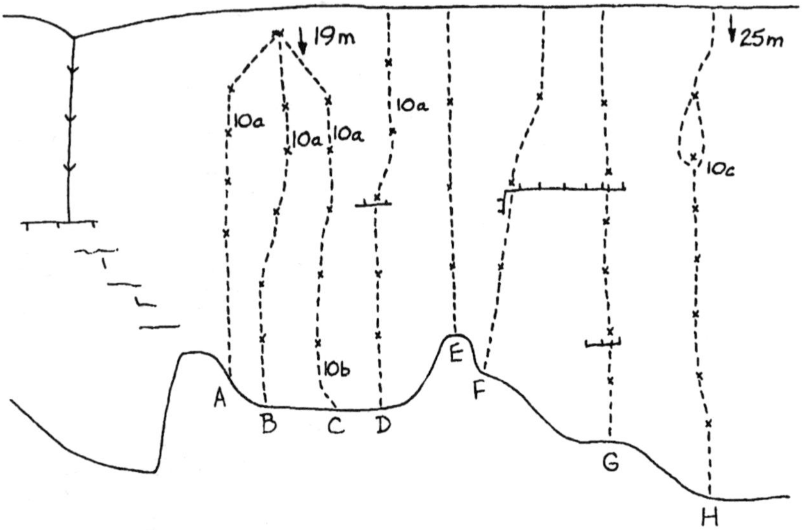


## HOODOO CRAG

| | | |
|---|---|---|
| A | Hoodlum * | 10a |
| B | Hoodunit ** | 10a |
| C | Hoodini * | 10b |
| D | Hoodoo You Love? ** | 10a |
| E | Deadly Buds | 10b |
| F | Hoor Tour | 10d |
| G | Who Are You? | 11b |
| H | Hoodoo Voodoo *** | 10c |

# STEVE CANYON

Steve Canyon is the next watercourse east of Grotto Canyon. This scenic and easily accessible little area is seldom visited by climbers, but it does have a few worthwhile routes. Take a few small wired nuts and Friends, as well as some webbing to tie into trees. One rope is sufficient to descend from any of the climbs, except *Dream Weaver* and *Take Five.*

**Approach**

Park north of Highway 1A at Grotto Pond Day Use Area, 2.4 km east of Gap Lake. Walk west along the Grotto Canyon hiking trail for a couple of minutes up a short incline, and then turn right at a watercourse. (If there is no room to park at the day use area, drive a short distance west to the Baymag Plant #2 sign. Follow a gravel road north about 150m and park where it intersects the trail to Grotto Canyon. From here, head east up the trail for a couple of minutes to reach the watercourse.) Follow the watercourse uphill for 10-15 minutes past a picturesquely sculptured waterslide to reach the Bathtub Crags, which sport a waterfall at the far end. The Upper Wall lies above the waterfall and can be reached as shown on the Bathtub Crags topo.

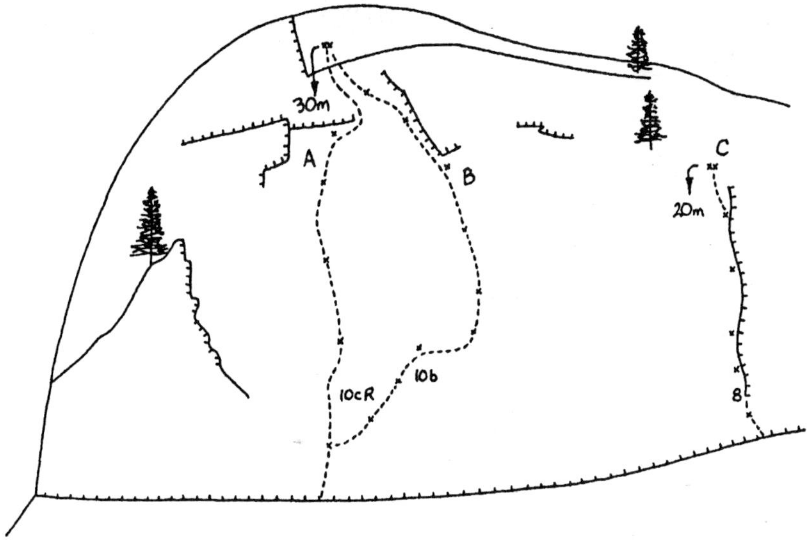


## UPPER WALL

| | | |
|---|---|---|
| A | Dream Weaver | 10c (R) |
| B | Take Five ** | 10b |
| C | Friendly Persuasion * | 8 |

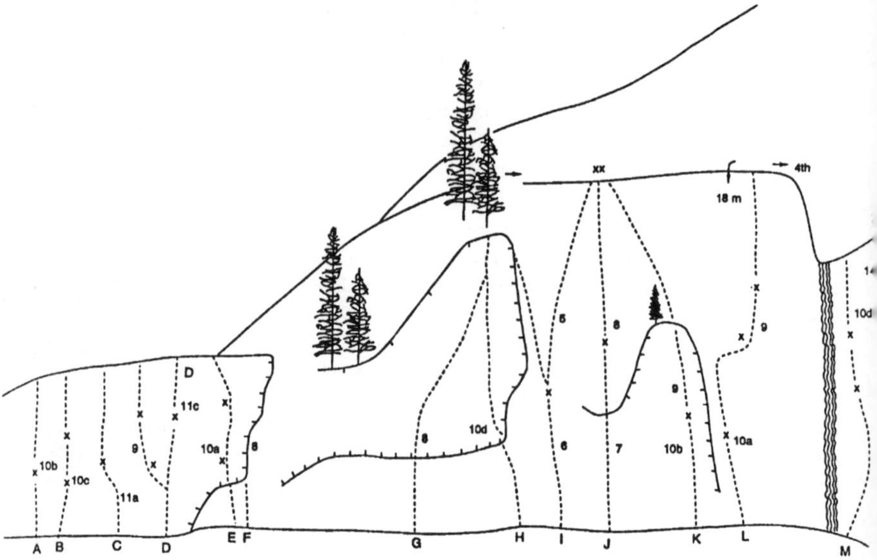


## BATHTUB CRAGS

| | | | |
|---|---|---|---|
| A | Pumpkin Smasher | 10b | RP3 |
| B | Where's the Beef? * | 10c | |
| C | Bermuda Triangle | 11a | |
| D | Tickicide * | 9 | |
| D' | Tickicide Direct | 10c | |
| E | Dr. Tongue's 3D House of Beef | 10a | |
| F | Poopy Corner | 8 | Friend 1.5 |
| G | Bozoids from Planet X | 5.8 | |
| H | Octopoids from the Deep | 10d | toprope |
| I | Kaka Corner | 6 | gear |
| J | Deadhead | 8 | |
| K | The Hump * | 10b | |
| L | The Devil Drives ** | 10a | |
| M | Moist and Easy *** | 10d | gear |

# KID GOAT AND NANNY GOAT

Kid Goat is the southernmost and smallest of the east-facing cliffs on the south ridge of Goat Mountain, the prominent peak that forms the mountain front immediately left (southwest) of Yamnuska. Nanny Goat is the next cliff right (north) of Kid Goat. The climbs covered in this guidebook are on a steep wall near the right (north) end of Kid Goat and in two small areas near the left (south) end of Nanny Goat. Both cliffs offer a unique style of climbing on good quality, remarkably prickly rock. Most of the climbs require a good selection of Rocks and Friends, and nearly all require two ropes to descend. With only one exception, the anchors on both cliffs were originally equipped with 11mm rope slings rather than chains, so it is probably a good idea to carry some webbing and a pocket knife in case it is necessary to replace the existing slings. A few routes are listed as "not recommended" because they require pitons. Because of their orientation, the cliffs warm up early in the morning but go out of the sun in early afternoon. It is also worth noting that they seep badly for a couple of days after rain.

**Approach**

Park at a paved pull-off on the south side of Highway 1A about 3.3 km west of the Highway 1X junction. Cross the highway and follow a gravel road to a landfill site (650 m). Walk through the landfill, or skirt around it on the right, to pick up a narrow gravel road on the far right (northwest) corner. Follow the road for about a minute to a fork. Follow the left fork to a small gravel pit and then continue up a fainter, steeper road a couple of minutes to a faint trail leading right. Follow this trail through a short section of forest to the watercourse that descends from the gully between Kid Goat and Nanny Goat. The trail now turns straight uphill, following first the left (south) side of the watercourse and then the right (north) side, and eventually reaching Nanny Goat near the gully. The *Predator* Area is immediately to the right. To reach *Overnight Sensation,* continue north past *Predator* for a few minutes along a sketchy trail near the base of the cliffs and then cross a short scree slope below a very prominent pale gray streak (the Great White Hope) to a small, south-facing facet of waterworn rock. To reach the Kid Goat climbs, turn left just before reaching Nanny Goat, cross the gully, and follow a trail at the base of the cliffs, first up a short wooded incline and then partway down the other side. If you have trouble getting oriented, the big, easily-recognized right-facing corner of *Smoking Mirror* is a good place to start.

Although it is possible to take a more direct route to the Kid Goat climbs than the one described here, please don't. The vegetation on this slope is very fragile and easily damaged; furthermore, the time saving is insignificant.

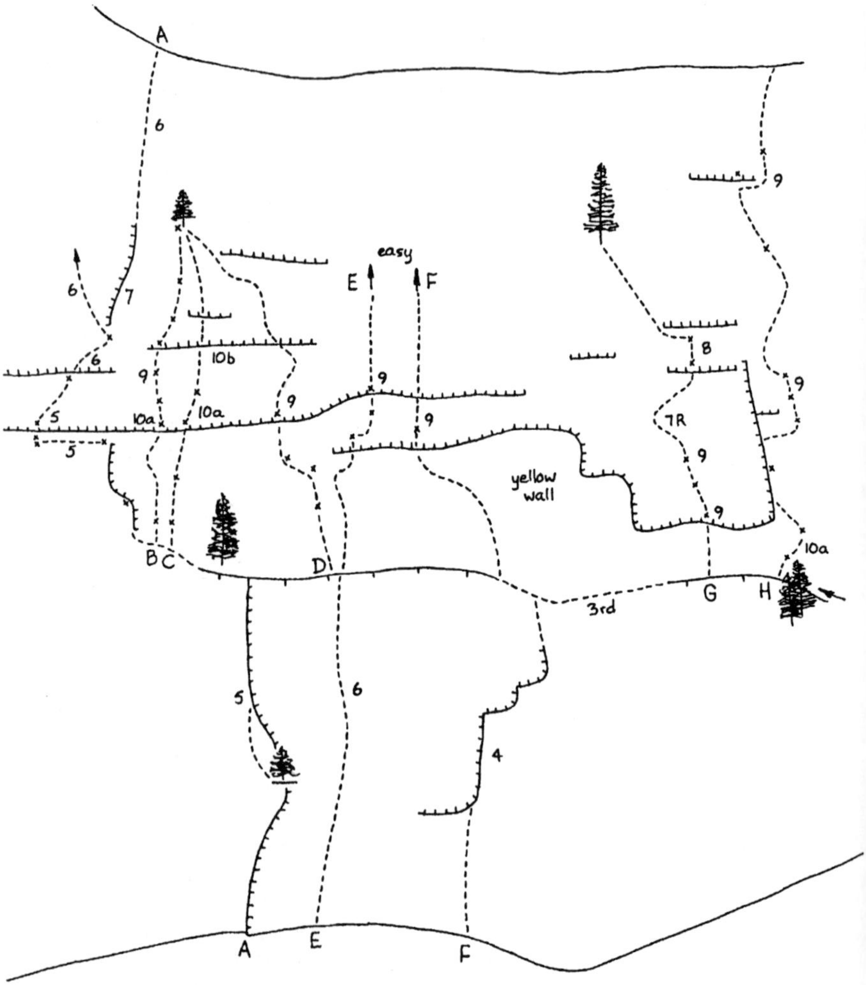


## KID GOAT, COARSE AND JUGGY AREA

| | | | |
|---|---|---|---|
| A | Twilight ** | 6 or 7 | gear to Friend 3.5 |
| B | True Stories ** | 10a/b | |
| C | Lies and Whispers ** | 10b | Rocks 1-4, Friend 4 |
| D | Coarse and Juggy ** | 9/10a | wired nuts |
| E | Dawntreader | 9 | not recommended |
| F | The Swell | 9 | not recommended |
| G | Half Life * | 9 | optional medium wired nut |
| H | Smoking Mirror *** | 10a | Rocks 1-8, Friends 1/2-4 |

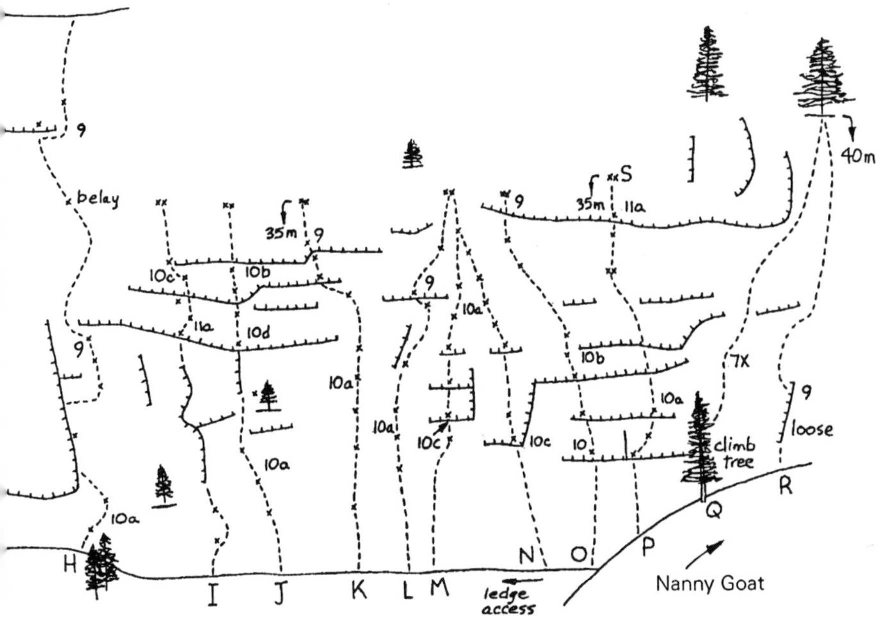


## KID GOAT, FEEDING FRENZY AREA

| | | | |
|---|---|---|---|
| H | Smoking Mirror *** | 10a | Rocks to #8, Friends 1/2-4 |
| I | Wave Goodbye *** | 11a | small wired nuts, Friends 1&3 |
| J | Max Headroom *** | 10d | |
| K | New Hope for the Dead **** | 10a | Friend 1.5 |
| L | Talk Dirty to Me *** | 10a | Rock 1, Friends 3.5-4 |
| M | Takedown *** | 10c | Friend 2 |
| N | Feeding Frenzy **** | 10c | optional Rock 5 |
| O | Divers from the Anaerobic Zone ** | 10b | optional RP 3 or 4 |
| P | Shakedown * | 10a | gear to Friend 3 |
| Q | Sticky Fingers | 7 (X) | not recommended |
| R | Slow Hand | 9 | not recommended |
| S | Breakdown ** | 11a | above P |

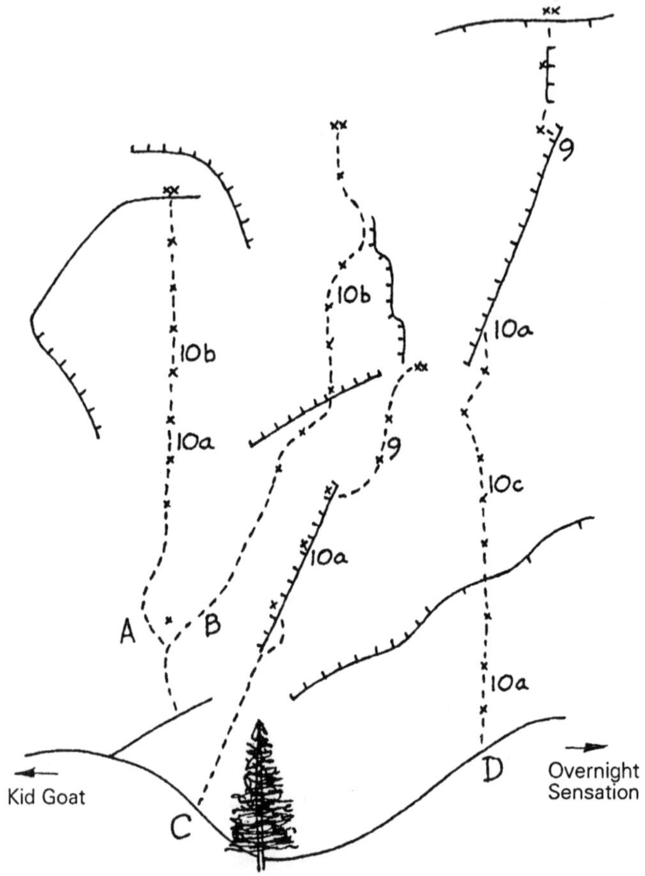


## NANNY GOAT, PREDATOR AREA

| | | | |
|---|---|---|---|
| A | Peep Show *** | 10b | |
| B | Blue Movie ** | 10b | Rocks 1-2 |
| C | Fadeout * | 10a | Rock 3 |
| D | Predator **** | 10c | Rocks 1-8, Friends 1-4 |

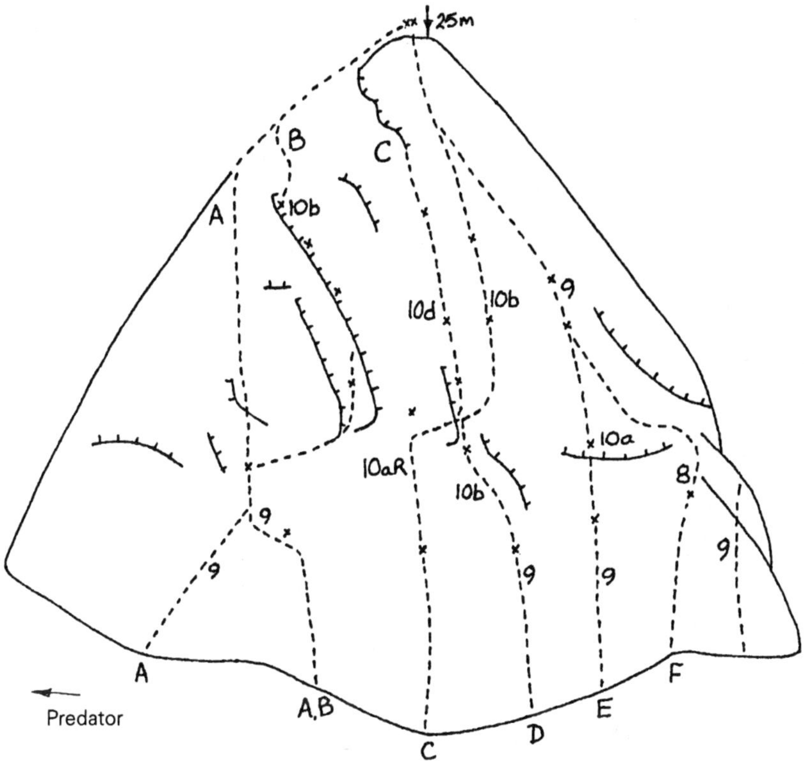


## OVERNIGHT SENSATION

| | | | |
|---|---|---|---|
| A | Nightland * | 9 | small Rocks |
| B | Bedtime Story ** | 10b | |
| C | Overnight Sensation * | 10d R | |
| D | Into the Night * | 10b | |
| D/C | Night Sensation *** | 10d | |
| E | Evening Star * | 10a | |
| F | Nightcap | 9 | Friend 1.5 |

# YAMNUSKA, CMC WALL

The route climbs the steep face just to the left of the summit of Yamnuska. Although it is not a sport climb, CMC Wall has recently been upgraded and as a result has more (and better) fixed protection than any other traditional route in the Bow Corridor. It is without a doubt the best route by far on Yamnuska and is thought by many to be the best multi-pitch rock climb in the Rockies; as such it should not be missed by those willing to wear a helmet, place a bit of protection and run it out a little bit more than on other climbs in this guide. Originally climbed as a mixed aid and free route by Billy Davidson and Urs Kallen in 1972, it was first free climbed by Bill Stark and Brian Wallace in 1984. Andy Genereux added variation pitches in 1987 and 1992. In 1990, he and Jon Jones rapped down the route on 100m ropes, installing double bolt belays and selectively replacing aid rivets with 3/8" bolts. The alternative pitches to the original pitches 4,5 and 6 are recommended. Take a full set of TCU's, RP's and Rocks, and Friends to #3. Using double ropes lessens rope drag and makes retreat possible.

**Approach**

Take the quarry access road, which leaves Highway 1A 2.1 km east of the junction with Highway 1X, to its end (1km). Walk through the quarry and follow a well used trail which zig-zags steeply up the slope to the base of Mt Yamnuska (40-50 minutes). Follow the trail left (west) along the base of the cliff for about 5 minutes until it is possible to scramble up scree gullies to the start of Calgary Route (the prominent left-slanting gash, left of the summit, which is clearly visible from the parking area). Traverse right 15 m, then scramble up 25 m to the top of a broad buttress. A careful search may turn up an old bolt, which marks the start of the climb. The usual descent, a walk-off, is to the west.

## YAMNUSKA

CMC Wall **** 11a

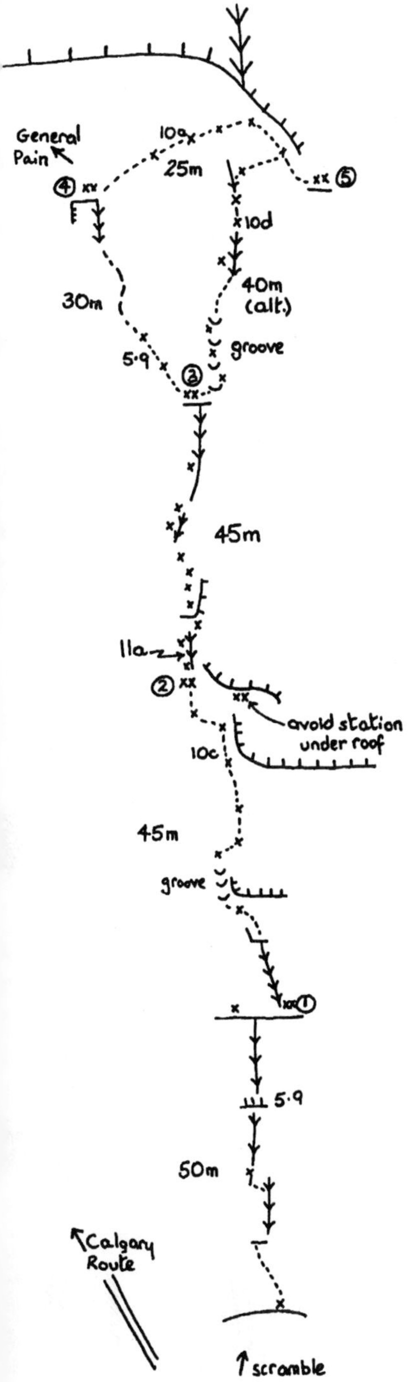


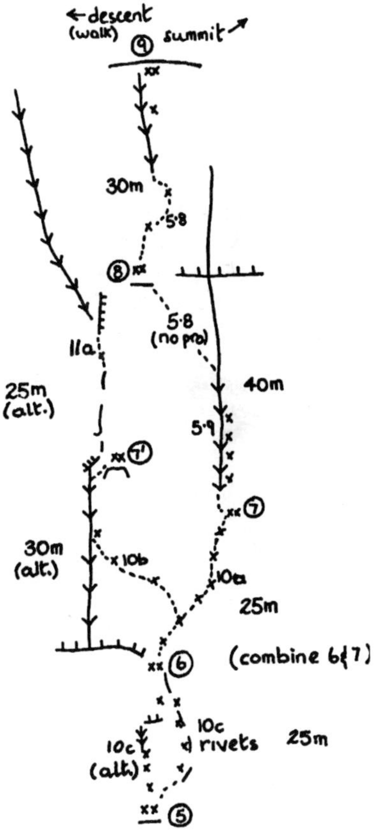

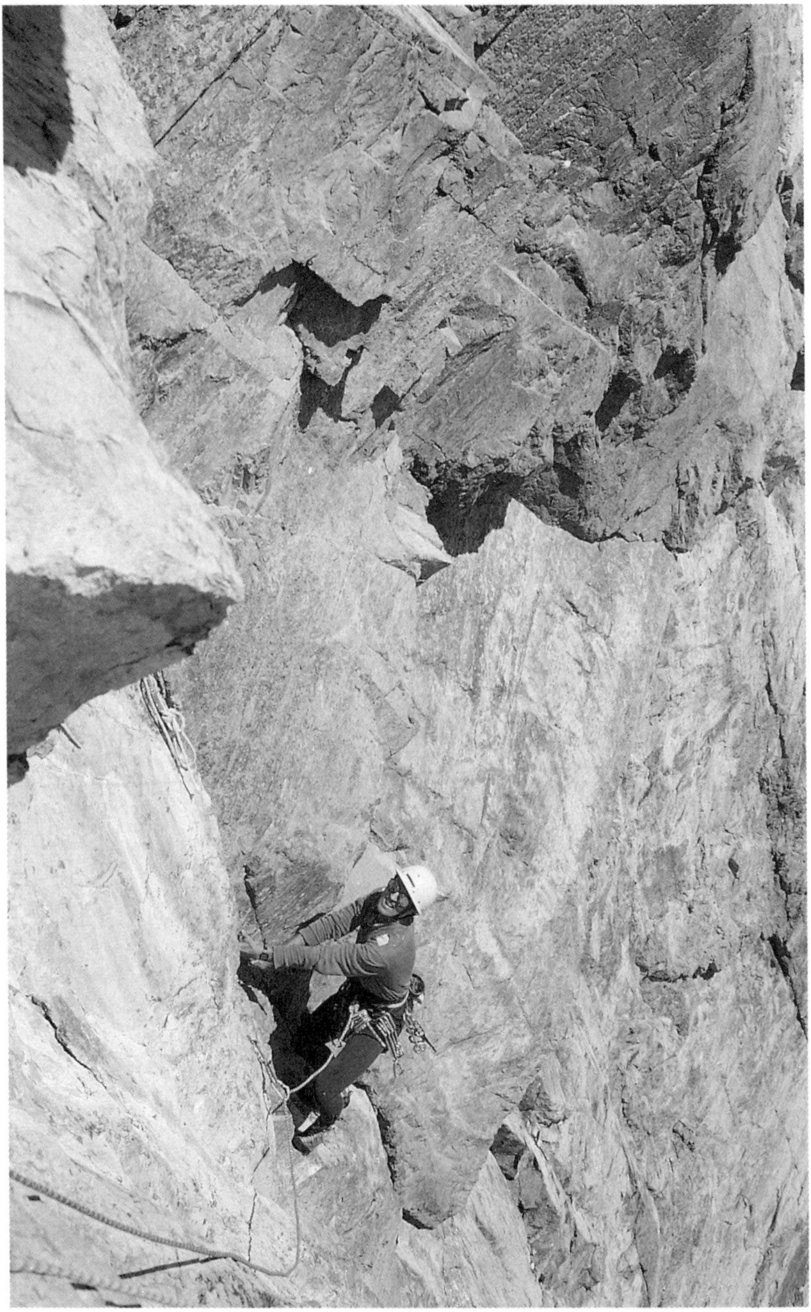

*Jon Jones on 2nd pitch of CMC Wall (11a), photo Andy Genereux*

# GRADED LIST OF ROUTES

**6**

Choc-a-Bloc *
Flake Line
Kaka Corner
Twilight **

**7**

Breezin' *
Jackorner **
Sticky Fingers
Toucha Toucha Me
Twilight var.**
Yet Another

**8**

Bozoids from Planet X
Cakewalk *
Cosmic String **
Dandelions *
Deadhead
Fat City *
Friendly Persuasion *
Heartline
Hockey Night in Canada *
Joyride *
Less Than Zero
Little Canadian Corner *
Nymphet **
OK Corral **
Poopy Corner
Potentilla Pillar
Rock 101 *
Yonge Street

**9**

Access Line, The
Baby Buoux *
Back to Zero
Blockhead
Burning Chrome **
Call of the Wild *
Callisto ***
Cameo **
Canary in a Coal Mine
Catspaw **
Cavebird
Chisum Trail
Dark Chocolate
Dawntreader
Dr. Watson
Empty Nest
Falling from Heaven ***
Girl Muscles *
Grime and Punishment *
Half Life *
Heart and Sole
Heartburn
Hollow Earth *
Ill Wind
Islands in the Stream **
Kinesthesia **
Loki **
Midden, The
Moriarty
Navigator
Nightcap
Nightland *
Oh No Not Another
Open Season *
Pining Away **
Rising Damp
Scavenger **
Scheherazade **
Sideline ***
Slow Hand
Sole Food
Swell, The
Tickicide *
Timeline **
Tiny Tim
Turning Shadows ***
Walk the Line *
Wild Horses
Yellow Wedge **

**9/10a**

Aqualung **
Burmese **
Coarse and Juggy **
Last Call *
Layla **
Swan Lake

**10a**

Abilene **
All Spruced Up **
American Graffiti **
Argon **
Art of the Ancients ***
Artful Dodger *
Banana Republic *
Basic Black *
Blaster *
Book Worm *
Brown Sugar *
Catseye **
Catspaw Direct *
Clip Trip **
Copromancer
Crybaby **
Dead Flowers *
Deviant Behaviour
Devil Drives, The
Dirty Work *
Dr. Tongue's 3D House of Beef
Double Header ***
Entrance Exam *
Entropy *
Evening Star *
Fadeout *
Feel on Baby ***
Grand Illusion **
Hoodlum *
Hoodoo You Love? **
Hoodunit **
Impending Impact ***
Impulse *
Innuendo
Kali **
Knight Shift
Lost World
Mickey Mantle
Monterey *
Mr. Percival *
Neuromancer **
New Hope for the Dead ****
Pink Cadillac ***
Redshift *
Riff Raff
Riparian **
Runaway
Sentinel, The **
Shakedown *
Sleeping Dog **
Slow Turning **
Smoking Mirror ***
Solarium *
Spring Clean *
Sticky Fingers Direct
Talk Dirty to Me ***
Tapdance *

Temerity
Tennessee Plates **
Venus ****
Watusi Wedding ****

### 10a/b

Soft Option **
Jugthuggery ***
True Stories **
Xanadu ***

### 10b

April Fool *
Bedtime Story **
Big Bang Theory **
Blackheart **
Blik *
Blue Movie **
Boy Scout Fundraiser *
Brontes **
Burnt Weenie Sandwich *
Byzantium ****
Cabin Fever **
Cafe Rambo *
California Dreaming
Caught in the Crossfire ***
Continental Drift **
Coprophobia **
Count Zero
Covert Action
Cro Magnon ***
Dead Heat
Deadly Buds
Deep Cover **
Diamond Sky
Diptheria
Divers from the Anaerobic Zone **
Educational Process **
Enchantress, The **
Evolution **
Face Value ****
Fire Extinguisher
For Your Eyes Only *
French Made
Gondwanaland **
Guitarzan *
Heart Crack
Hey Presto ***
Holey Redeemer ***
Hoodini *
Hotwire**
Hump, The
Into the Night **
Jack of Clubs *
Jesus Drives a Cadillac **
Law and Order **
Lemon Pie **
Lies and Whispers **
Lunch Rambo Style **
Merlin's Laugh (alt.) ****
Merlin's Laugh (p 2) **
Moonabago
Nine to Five **
Peep Show ***
Penguin Lust ****
Pitrun **
Pumpkin Smasher
Rock 201 *
Run of the River ***
Search Pattern ***
Serenade **
Shadowland**
So It's a Sport Climb ****
Strandline **
Summertime Blues (p1) ***
Supplication *
Take Five **
Tempest, The *****
Thrushold **
True Grit ***
True Stories **
Under Cover ***
Up the Creek **
Wetback **
Weird Noises **

### 10b/c

Squirrel Breath ***

### 10c

Ablutor, The **
Away From It All ***
Bob's Yer Uncle ***
Breathless **
Cat and Mouse **
Chameleon *
Coconut Joe *
Conifer Crack ***
Cloak and Dagger **
Critical Mass ****
Dirty Trick
Dream Weaver
Double Cross**
Equinox **
Fast Forward *
Feeding Frenzy ****
Free Lunch ***
George of the Jungle ***
Grander Illusion, The ***
Gringo ***
Harder Than It Looks
Heatwave
History of Time **
Hollow Victory
Honky Tonk Woman *
Hoodoo Voodoo ***
Junior Woodchuck
Jamboree **
Lapidarist
Layaway Plan **
Left to Chance
Loose Lips Sink Ships
Lysdexia ***
Madame X*
Made in the Shade ***
Mainline *
Malibu *
Mandala ***
Midnight Rambler *
Mona Lisa Overdrive *
Pilot Error *
Power Play **
Predator ****
Prime Cut ****
Puppet on a Chain *
Raindust
Rat Patrol **
Rub Me Right
Scirocco ***
Sleight of Hand ***
Small Fry
Small Is Beautiful ***
Sticky Fingers ****
Stone Cold **
Superstition **
Takedown ***
Temptress ***
Tickicide Direct
Trading Places **
Under the Gun ****
Undertow **
Vandals in Babylon **
Verdict, The **
West Coast Idea *
When the Going Gets Weird ***
When Worlds Collide **
Where's the Beef? *
Whiplash **
X-terminator ***

**10c/d**

Aggressive Treatment **
Bite the Rainbow ***
Grand Larceny ***
Think Tall

**10d**

Aquacide *
Arcana ***
Archaos **
Baker Street
Block Buster ***
Bogus
Caveling
Cover-up **
Diving Board, The ***
Dynamic Dumpling ***
Excitable Boy ***
High Wire *
Hoor Tour
Indigo
Lip Service *
Lithium **
Max Headroom ***
Moist and Easy ***
Monkey Puzzle
Night Sensation ***
Octopoids from the Deep
Overnight Sensation *
Parallel Dreams ***
Party Line ***
Poolside Pleasures ****
Raven, The ***
Rocky & Me
Shockwave ****
Short and Curly *
Stiff Upper Lip *
Sting, The *
Summertime Blues (p2) **
Tabernaquered
Thrushold Direct **
Tree Men ****
Wise Guys ****

**10d/11a**

Fly By Wire *

**11a**

Accidental Tourist, The
Ashtaroth ***
Bermuda Triangle
Big Breasted Girls Go to the Beach and Take Their Tops Off ***
Black Magic ****
Blackheart Direct **
Breakdown **
CMC Wall ****
Canadian Air, pitch 1
Cold Shoulder
Cyberpunk ***
Delilah **
Electric Ocean *****
Facelift ****
Farewell to Arms *****
Fire Alarm
Footloose
Grand Delusion *
Grey Matter **
Hard Bodies *
Heart of Darkness ***
Heart of Gold
Heliopolis ***
Holey Redeemer Direct **
Island Experience *
It's Not the Length That Counts ***
Knight Moves *
K.P. Special
Last Word, The ***
Lunatic Madness
Mean Street **
Mendocino *
Merlin's Laugh (original start) ****
Midterm **
Monkey in a Rage **
Night Life **
Peter Pan
Problems With Guinness ****
Redshift Connection **
Runners on 'Roids **
Self Abuse *
Siren Song ***
Some Like It Hot **
Stormy Weather
Tender Mercies **
Wave Goodbye ***
Whistling in the Dark ***
Weird Turn Pro, The ***

**11a/b**

Dressed to Kill ***
Dynosoar **
Faux Pas ***
Gravity Rodeo ***
Leave Your Hat On, pitch 1
Phoenix, The ***
Surface Tension **

**11b**

110 in the Shade ****
Advanced Education **
Bandits at 2 O'clock ****
Bitch **
Bitter End ***
Bob's Direct ***
Capone ****
Chips Are for Kids ***
Comfortably Numb ***
Cultural Imperative ***
Engines Burning ***
Fear No Art ***
For Whom the Bell Tolls *
Hat Trick ***
Is That Your 'Dog? **
Last Gasp ***
Magic in the Air ***
Magus, The ***
No Sloppy Seconds ***
New Painted Lady, The *
Prince of Darkness **
Rough Trade **
Rush **
Salsa Inglesa *
Scarface
Sidewinder ***
Sorcerer's Apprentice, The ****
Stinkfinger **
Stolen Thunder (alt. finish)
Submission Direct ****
Tears of the Dinosaur *
Tilt **
Too Low for Zero *
Tour de Pump *
Underhanded Tactics **
Walk Don't Run **
Who Are You?
Wilt ****
Witches' Brew
Withering Heights ***
Young Guns *****
Younger Than Yesterday **

**11b/c**

Altered States **
Dr Tongue's 3D House of Slave Chicks **
Just Another John **
Moon Over Miami ***
Mr. Clean

**11c**

Across the River and into the Trees
Barchetta ****
Beach Balls
Bombs Away **
Caliburn ****
Cerebral Goretex
Chainsaw Wall
Dark Star ***
Danse Macabre **
Dayglo Rage ****
Demonstone **
Depth Charge *
Digital Stimulation ***
Fall Guy *
Feeling the Pinch **
Fly by Night **
High Octane **
Higher Learning ***
Hardest 5.8 in the Rockies, The ****
Hocus Pocus *
Illusionist, The ***
Lively Up Yourself
Love and Death
Mistral **
Natural Selection ***
Phlogiston ***
Power Hour ***
Quantum Physics **
Short Sword, The ***
Smear Campaign
Spider in a Tub ***
Stolen Thunder *
Summer in Siam ****
Suspended Sentence ****
Tower of Pisa **
Trinidad **
Walk on the Wilde Side *****
Why Shoot the Teacher? ***

**11c/d**

Blackened
Hush **
Klingon War **
Masque, The
Physical Graffiti ****
Silent Scream **
Subliminal Seduction **

**11d**

Abracadabra ****
Ancient Life
Both Guns Blazing **
Crossroad **
Grace Under Pressure ****
Hellen Damnation *
Irradiator, The
Learning the Game **
Mephisto ****
Mirage
Mr. Olympia **
Muscle Beach *****
Reflex Action
Repulse
Saigon Kiss ***
Stone Age Romeos ****
Submission ****
Sun City ***
Sunshine Boys **
Surfer Poser
Urban Youth
Wings of Desire **

**12a**

Chandelle **
Double Cross Direct *
Fine Print, The *
French Connection *
Girl Drink Drunk
Hummingbird Arete***
Illy Down
Importance of Being Ernest, The ****
Leave Your Hat On, p 2
Mighty Mite **
No More Mr. Nice Guy ****
Open Book Exam ***
Outer Limits ***
Path of the Moose *
Shadow of a Thin Man ****
Snakes and Ladders **
Success Pool ****
Tour de Force ****
Truckasaurus
Warlock, The *****
Wizard, The *****

**12a/b**

Brent's Big Birthday **
Canadian Air, pitch 2
I'm a Lazy Man

**12b**

Blue Lotus **
Dr. No **
Gizzard, The *****
Lizard, The **
Nothing Up My Sleeves *****
Third Degree Burn ***

**12b/c**

Cracked Rhythm **
Telltale Heart

**12c**

Stygian Ayre ***
Sword in the Stone, The **
Tropicana

**12c/d**

Cause and Effect
Crimes of Passion

**12d**

Slap Shot
Tintin and Snowy Get Psyched ****

**13a**

Metabolica ***
Nirvana
Shep's Diner

**13b**

American Standard ****
Burn Hollywood Burn
Resurrection, The

# INDEX